MISTY COPELAND

PRINCIPAL BALLERINA

Published in 2018 by Enslow Publishing, LLC.
101 W. 23rd Street, Suite 240, New York, NY 10011

Library of Congress Cataloging-in-Publication Data

Names: Staley, Erin, author.
Title: Misty Copeland : principal ballerina / Erin Staley.
Description: New York : Enslow Publishing, 2018. | Series: Influential Lives | Includes bibliographical references and index. | Audience: Grades: 7–12.
Identifiers: LCCN 2017003045 | ISBN 9780766085091 (library-bound)
Subjects: LCSH: Copeland, Misty—Juvenile literature. | Ballet dancers—United States—Biography—Juvenile literature. | African American dancers—Biography—Juvenile literature.
Classification: LCC GV1785.C635 S73 2018 | DDC 792.8092—dc23
LC record available at https://lccn.loc.gov/2017003045

Printed in the United States of America

To Our Readers: We have done our best to make sure all websites in this book were active and appropriate when we went to press. However, the author and the publisher have no control over and assume no liability for the material available on those websites or on any websites they may link to. Any comments or suggestions can be sent by email to customerservice@enslow.com.

Photo Credits: Cover, pp. 1, 55 J. Countess/Getty Images; pp. 4, 17, 39, 76, 98 © AP Images; p. 9 Bettmann/Getty Images; pp. 26–27 Portland Press Herald/Getty Images; p. 30 Frederick M. Brown /Getty Images; p. 32 Ali Burafi/AFP/Getty Images; p. 44 Boston Globe/Getty Images; p. 48 ZUMA Press, Inc./Alamy Stock Photo; pp. 52–53 Thomas Barwick/Stone/Getty Images; pp. 60–61 Hiroyuki Ito/Hulton Archive/Getty Images; p. 63 © Buchan/Rex Shutterstock/ZUMA Press; p. 66 Kevin Mazur/WireImage/Getty Images; pp. 68, 78–79, 92–93 PR NEWSWIRE/AP; pp. 70–71 White House Photo/Alamy Stock Photo; p. 74 The Washington Post/Getty Images; p. 86 Grant Lamos IV/ FilmMagic/Getty Images; p. 87 Larry Busacca/Getty Images; p. 95 Bruce Glikas/FilmMagic/Getty Images; pp. 106–107 Gabriel Olsen/FilmMagic/Getty Images; back cover and interior pages background graphic zffoto/Shutterstock.com.

Contents

CHAPTER ONE

A Ballerina Is Born

T o watch Misty Copeland dance is to watch power, precision, and elegance command the stage. Her dancing seems effortless, thanks to endless hours spent training, rehearsing, performing, and touring. Copeland makes it look easy, but easy is not what her journey has been to fulfill her dream of becoming a principal dancer for the American Ballet Theatre (ABT). She has overcome personal challenges, broken through barriers, and advocated for diversity— all with the intent of sharing the beauty and possibility of ballet.

Joining the Copeland Company

Misty Danielle Copeland was born to Sylvia

> "It took Misty Copeland only twenty years to become an overnight success." [1]

As a young dancer, Misty Copeland found the discipline she longed for in her life. She fell in love with dance and worked hard to rise through the ranks to become a principal dancer.

DelaCerna and Doug Copeland on September 10, 1982. She was the youngest of four siblings (Erica, Doug Jr., and Chris) in her Kansas City, Missouri, home. DelaCerna was a former Kansas City Chiefs cheerleader. Her children thought she looked like the famous five-octave singer Mariah Carey. Like Carey, DelaCerna is biracial. She had an Italian mother and an African American father. But unlike Carey, DelaCerna didn't know her parents. As a child, an African American couple adopted DelaCerna. They died when she was a young girl, and DelaCerna stayed with various relatives. She was often left to raise herself.

Right after high school, DelaCerna married a man named Mike. The newlyweds moved to Oakland, California. However, Mike experienced a fatal gunshot. DelaCerna mourned the loss alongside his best friend, Doug Copeland. He, too, is biracial, with a German mother and an African American father. DelaCerna and Copeland married and went on to have four children.[2]

Life with Harold

DelaCerna left Doug Copeland when Misty was two years old. She loaded the children onto a bus headed across the country to Bellflower, California. It took two days to reach the Los Angeles suburb. DelaCerna and her children lived with Harold, a man DelaCerna had known from childhood. He eventually became her third husband and the biological father to Misty's younger sister, Lindsey.

Harold was fun loving, kind, and a bit of a prankster. Misty would often sit with him on the sofa and share sunflower seeds. He'd also make waffles and cozy up on the sofa with Misty and Lindsey to watch Saturday morning cartoons. Misty considered Harold to be her father, not having remembered Doug Copeland. And while the children only saw the lighthearted side of Harold, he was an alcoholic. The effects of his drinking frightened DelaCerna. Five years later, she packed up her station wagon—kids and all. As an adult, Copeland remembers the positive impact Harold had on her life. By the time she wrote her 2014 memoir, *Life in Motion: An Unlikely Ballerina*, Harold had been in recovery for nearly two decades.[3]

A New Home, A New Stepfather

DelaCerna drove her children—who now totaled five—to San Pedro. This charming community in Los Angeles, California, is located next to Los Angeles Harbor. It is an area that relies heavily on the fishing trade. Robert, a radiologist of mixed Asian ethnicity, received them. He would become DelaCerna's fourth husband and the biological father to Misty's younger brother, Cameron. Robert was very different from Harold in both personality and expectations. Robert required the children to do chores, such as taking out the garbage, sweeping after breakfast, and doing the dishes. It was the first time they'd ever had such responsibilities.[4]

As the children grew, they began developing their own personalities and strong suits. Erica, Misty's twelve-year-old sister, took on a parenting role. She combed and dried Misty's hair, and walked her siblings to school. As an adult, she would have her own family. Doug Jr. was an avid reader and later worked in insurance. Chris, who had a lot of energy and showed no fear, was an athlete and future lawyer. Lindsey, with her father's sense of humor and her mother's smile, later earned a track scholarship at Chico State University. Cameron, the son of Sylvia and Robert, later became a piano prodigy. And while they all had their own interests, they shared a love for sports. They often gathered around the television to watch the Chicago Bulls, the San Francisco 49ers, and of course, the Kansas City Chiefs![5]

Mesmerized by Movement

Misty wasn't as much of a sports fan as her brothers and sisters, but there was one star athlete that caught her attention: Nadia Comaneci. At seven years old, Misty watched a Lifetime movie of the Romanian gymnast dominate 1976 Summer Olympics in Montreal, Canada. At the time, Nadia was fourteen years old, and she became the first gymnast in Olympic history to score a perfect 10.0. Misty recorded the movie on her VCR and watched it again and again. She was especially drawn to the floor routines, with their elements of dance and gymnastics. The movements were not only graceful but

Nadia Comaneci, An Olympic Champion

At age fourteen, at the 1976 Montreal Olympics, Romanian Nadia Comaneci became the first gymnast to score a perfect 10.0. By the end of the competition, she had earned seven perfect tens. This monumental achievement gave her three gold medals, one bronze, and one silver. Four years later, Comaneci returned to the Olympics. This time it was in Moscow, Russia. She earned two gold and two silver medals,

Nadia Comaneci became a worldwide sensation in 1976. More than a decade later, a movie about the Olympic champion caught the attention of a young Misty Copeland.

bringing her Olympic total to nine. In 1996, Comaneci was inducted into the International Gymnastics Hall of Fame. Three years later, ABC News and Ladies' Home Journal named her one of the 100 Most Important Women of the 20th Century.

Today, Comaneci travels the world, speaking at engagements and promoting health and fitness. She serves as the vice-chairperson of the board of directors of Special Olympics International, a vice president of the Muscular Dystrophy Association, and a board member for the Laureus Sports for Good Foundation.[7]

powerful. Misty tried to re-create routines from what she saw on the movie. She turned cartwheels, stood on her hands, and performed back walkovers, just like her newfound hero.[6]

Bouts with Anxiety

Misty was a quiet middle child, eager to please, and all too happy to blend in. She was nervous, worried, and preoccupied with being perfect. She didn't want to disappoint anyone, especially her mother. With so many children in her family, it was difficult to get her mother's attention. She didn't have much of a voice, and the combination of it all gave her anxiety.[8]

Migraines plagued Misty, as they had her mother when she was Misty's age. Sometimes the pain was so severe that Misty had to leave school early. Light and sound worsened the pain, and to recover, she would lay in a dark, quiet room. Misty's anxiety was always heightened at school. She never liked to be called on, and she did everything possible to avoid criticism, embarrassment, and exposure in front of her peers.

One summer, Misty pleaded with her mother to let her visit her new middle school early so she could pre-determine the route to her classes. She was worried that she would get lost in the new school and would arrive late to class. Her mother told her to relax, and

Anxiety 101

Anxiety is a reaction to a danger or threat. It works as an internal alarm and sends a rush of adrenaline through the body. Adrenaline is a hormone that is a part of the fight-flight response. It's a natural physical response that helps the body fight against danger or flee if needed. Adrenaline makes the heart speed up and quickens breathing.

Anxiety can range from mild to intense. Mild anxiety can occur if someone is nervous, uneasy, or always on alert. Intense anxiety occurs when one feels fear, panic, or dread of what might or will happen. Anxiety is common, and it affects people of all ages in all sorts of ways. One could experience a queasy stomach, tense muscles, trembling limbs, and difficulty sleeping. Intense headaches, called migraines, can cause problems with vision, vomitting, and sensitivities to light, sound, and smell.[9]

let it go. But Misty couldn't let it go. Although her mother didn't let Misty map out a route that year, she did do it before she entered high school. Misty went ahead of time, figured out the route, and once school was in session, arrived an hour early to her first class. This was all because of her anxiety of getting lost and being late. But she made good use of her time: Misty sat on the floor in front of her locker and studied until class began.

Music provided solace in the family home, especially for Misty. She frequently played CDs or tape cassettes of her favorite musicians. Popular choices included TLC, Toni Braxton, New Edition, MC Hammer, and LL Cool J. Mariah Carey was always at the top of the family's playlist. They considered Carey's debut album to be their soundtrack. It even soothed baby Cameron's crying. For Misty, though, Carey's music inspired dance. She would retreat to a bedroom, turn up the volume, and choreograph routines to the lyrics. Her movements mimicked what she saw the pop star perform in her music videos.[10]

An Introduction to Racial Bigotry

With Robert, Misty and her family lived in a beautiful house. Healthy food was on the table, and nice clothes were on their backs. Books and toys kept them entertained, and they learned some household skills, such as cooking. Misty even helped Robert with errands, which won his favor. Robert's mother taught her how to sew, and she used her newfound skill to make outfits for her dolls.

But life with Robert was not all fun and games. He was a new husband and father to five children, and he was often overwhelmed. He relied on his own strict upbringing, which was sometimes accompanied by physical punishment from his father. Manners were imperative, and peace and quiet were mandatory. (Oddly enough, the structure seemed to calm Misty's anxiety.) Expectations were high, even for Misty with her people-pleasing nature and resemblance to his family. Robert thought of her as his "little Hawaiian girl," a sharp contrast to the darker tones of her siblings. If rules were broken, or the house was way too rambunctious, the offending party was made to stand in the corner. The boys had it worse. They were either hit or made to stand in the corner for an hour with a heavy book on their heads. It was hard for Misty to watch. As Robert's frustration mounted, he encouraged physical violence. When the boys had disagreements, he'd wrap their fists with rags and order them to "duke it out" out. He also made racial slurs and jokes at their expense. It was the first time Misty had been exposed to racial bigotry. The children began hiding whenever Robert was around, and they would hole themselves up in a bedroom to be together and listen to music.

Sylvia and Robert's marriage was falling apart. Robert abused her, physically and verbally. She told the children to ready themselves. She was planning an exit. When the day finally came, a man named Ray helped DelaCerna pack up the children. They left Robert for good.[11]

Life in Flux

DelaCerna and her children temporarily stayed in a welcoming but poorly located home in downtown Los Angeles. It was in gang territory. Misty and her siblings were very scared, as shootings were commonplace in the neighborhood. They eventually moved in with their mother's new boyfriend, Ray. It was short-lived, though. They then moved to Montebello and lived in a small apartment with Alex, DelaCerna's next boyfriend. Their family life was in flux, and the children longed for stability. They grew bitter and wanted their mother to focus on them rather than on the man at her side. They stuck together, though, taking care of one another.

Money was extremely tight for Misty and her family. DelaCerna had been trained as a nurse in Kansas City but switched to sales when she moved to California. Sales is known to be a tough industry as salespeople often work on commission. They don't get paid unless a sale is made. This can cause commissions to be good one month and not so good the next. This was the case for DelaCerna. Eventually, she was out of work. She lost her car, and Alex lost the apartment. The family then moved into a welfare motel in Gardena, California. It was called the Sunset Inn, and it was very shabby. Its large front room was where the children slept, either on the floor or sofa. Alex and DelaCerna shared the single bedroom. Food stamps bought the groceries, and sometimes the family had to search between the sofa cushions for extra spending money. Embarrassed by her family's living conditions, Misty withdrew. She lost herself in her schoolwork and, later, in her dance lessons.[12]

CHAPTER TWO

Becoming a "Bun Head"

· · · · · · · · · · · · · · · · · ·

Misty Copeland first stepped onto the stage at the age of five. Her mother had entered her into her elementary school's talent show. Her sister, Erica, and brother Chris joined her on stage. They danced to the Marvelette's 1961 song "Please Mr. Postman." They spent weeks practicing after school. In homemade costumes, they took the stage with confidence. Misty ate up the applause and especially her mother's praise. DelaCerna was so proud and told Misty that she belonged on stage.[1]

Finding a Voice

As a middle schooler, Misty auditioned for the school's prize-winning drill team. Her sister Erica had been a star member of the team. Misty admired her talent and beauty, and wanted to be just like her. Misty wanted not only to be on the team but also to become its captain. To do so, she was required to audition two routines: one with the team and the other as a self-choreographed solo. Misty chose her own music. Erica helped with the choreography, and Misty rehearsed daily. Her hard work paid off. She not only made the team but also became captain.

Misty's middle school achievements continued. She became the sixth grade treasurer and a hall monitor. By getting involved in school activities, Misty began to find her voice. She was no longer the shy middle child. She was popular, despite being the youngest and the smallest dancer on the team.[2]

Gaining Skills

The drill team's coach, Elizabeth "Liz" Cantine, had received classical ballet training as a child. She used some of this know-how in her drill team practices and choreography. The skills were basic and easy enough for the dancers to pick up. Misty used them in the routines she choreographed for the team. One holiday, she put it all together—plus a kickline—to Mariah Carey's 1994 song, "All I Want for Christmas Is You." She also put her sewing skills to work by making red skirts trimmed in faux fur. They were to go with the team's new red leotards. For props, Misty wrapped red canes that had been used in a past holiday show with white tape. The team spent weekends rehearsing, and when performance day came, they were received with a standing ovation.[3]

A Life-Changing Introduction

Liz Cantine believed that Misty had the ideal dancer's body. At 4 feet (1.2 meters) tall and 70 pounds (31.8 kilograms), Misty was petite. She had a small head, long neck, short torso, and long legs—the perfect ballerina body according to legendary ballet master George Balanchine. Like DelaCerna, Cantine thought that Misty had natural talent. She wanted the youngster to meet her friend and former ballerina Cynthia "Cindy" Bradley.

As a teenager, Bradley had danced professionally for several companies, including the Virginia Ballet Company and the Louisville Ballet. An injury ended her professional career, and Bradley became a ballet teacher. She opened the San Pedro Dance Center in Palos Verdes, California, with her husband, Patrick, an artist-dancer.

Ballet instructor Cynthia Bradley (shown above) recognized something special in Misty Copeland. She invited the young dancer to live with her to focus on her ballet training. It was during this time that the very shy girl found her voice through ballet.

As community outreach, Bradley taught free classes at the Boys & Girls Club in San Pedro. It was the same Boys & Girls Club that Misty and her siblings went to every day after school. In fact, they just had to walk two blocks to get there, and after participating in classes and activities, they caught a ride home with their mother. By teaching at the Boys & Girls Club, Bradley hoped to find dance talent in her classes. She wanted to connect with students who not only had potential but who also had a passion to study ballet more seriously.[4]

From the Bleachers to the Barre

Not wanting to disappoint Coach Cantine, Misty reluctantly crept into the gym to watch Bradley's ballet class. Misty sat in the bleachers, hoping not to be noticed. This pattern continued for about a week or so until Bradley approached her. The teacher asked Misty to join them, but the youngster wasn't ready quite yet. Plus, she didn't have the proper leotard and ballet slippers the other students wore. Misty continued to observe from the bleachers for another week, and when she finally worked up enough courage to make her way to the barre, she wore a T-shirt, long cotton shorts, and gym socks.

When class was over, Misty was ready to quit. She couldn't relate to this classical dance form. It wasn't anything like her drill team rehearsals. Misty dodged the class after that, but her avoidance didn't go unnoticed. About a week later, Bradley called Misty to join her at the front of the class. Misty was confused and self-conscious, but she did as was asked. Bradley began shaping Misty's body into traditional ballet positions. She even lifted the young girl's leg to her ear. Impressively, Misty was strong enough to hold it in that difficult position. It felt natural to Misty, and Bradley was elated. Never before had she encountered such a student! Misty began attending ballet class at the Boys & Girls Club regularly.[5]

Ballet Training Begins

Misty's dance training began with ballet basics. She learned the five positions of the feet, as well as arm placement and traveling steps. Many of these were first introduced at the barre and later executed with pirouettes (turns on one leg) and grand jetés (leaps in the air). Misty was

> "At thirteen, Copeland was still a child at heart, playing with Barbies in her free time."[7]

getting stronger, and her enthusiasm was growing. But she still had a great deal of "catching up" to do. In ballet, most dancers start training at the age of five or six. Misty's thirteen years were considered to be too old. She began to doubt herself and what she could accomplish. However, Bradley knew that with proper training, any lost time could be made up. All the thirteen-year-old needed was formal training.[6]

Bradley invited Misty to study at her studio, the San Pedro Dance Center. The only problem was that the ballet studio was about twenty-five minutes across town. In addition, Misty was still involved with the drill team. Bradley sent Misty home with letters to her mother, explaining that Bradley would like to invite Misty to study at her ballet school. The letters never made it home. Misty hid them or tossed them in the trash. She wasn't ready to leave the drill team. She still loved it, and the association it had to her mother and sister was strong.

When Bradley inquired about the letters, Misty made up all sorts of excuses. But Bradley persisted. Misty reluctantly gave the ballet teacher her home number. Bradley called Misty's mother and explained that she would offer Misty a full scholarship. She would even give Misty a ride to the studio every afternoon. DelaCerna knew it was a great opportunity for her daughter, and she agreed to the arrangement.[8]

Stepping into the Studio

Misty began her lessons at the San Pedro Dance Center. She wore her hair in a bun, a black leotard, pink tights, and soft leather ballet slippers to comfortably perform the intricate, and often quick, footwork. The San Pedro Dance Center was very different than the Boys & Girls Club. The studio was in a shopping center, and special dance flooring made it possible for students to dance full out in their ballet slippers without slipping. Mirrors hung on the walls, and a sound system amplified the classical music that played for each section of class. There was also a lack of diversity in the student population. Most of

George Balanchine

Georgi Melitonovich Balanchivadze was born in St. Petersburg, Russia, in 1904. He studied ballet, piano, and music theory. In 1921, he danced for the Mariinsky Theater. When he danced for Ballets Russes in Paris, he changed his name to George Balanchine.[10] He had choreographed ballets for various European companies when Lincoln Kirstein, a dance connoisseur, asked him to cofound a ballet school and company in the United States.

Balanchine arrived in New York City in 1933. The School of American Ballet opened in 1934, and professional company American Ballet began in 1935.[11] Balanchine's neoclassic influence, musicality, muses, and ballerina body preferences greatly impacted modern-day ballet. Some of his works include *Swan Lake*, *The Nutcracker*, *A Midsummer Night's Dream,* and *Don Quixote*. Balanchine also choreographed for Broadway and Hollywood, and went on to create and direct the New York City Ballet in 1948. Balanchine became a US citizen in 1939.[12]

these studio dancers were Caucasian, which was very different than what she'd experienced at the Boys & Girls Club. Bradley explained that the world of ballet had room for everyone. Even though her skin didn't match that of the others in her classes, Misty eventually made friends, and she began to feel powerful when she looked in the mirror.[9]

En Pointe

Ballet begins with the basics, with each movement and position building on the next. Because Misty was behind in her training, she took classes with students who were considerably younger than she. She fit right in thanks to her petite size. Misty mimicked what was taught, and she picked it up quickly. Bradley didn't take it easy on her young protégé. She put Misty in advanced classes, too, pushing her knowledge and facility. Misty worked hard and rose to the challenge.

Eight weeks into her training, she went en pointe. This means to dance on the tips of the toes while wearing pointe shoes. Pointe shoes allow the ballerina to appear as if she's dancing in the air. Going en pointe is an honor for any ballerina-in-training. It normally takes several years of consistent training to build up enough strength and technical understanding. For Misty to achieve this in just a few months was extraordinary.

Misty was set to perform en pointe for an art, music, and dance show at the Palos Verdes Art Center in Rancho Palos Verdes, California. Bradley created the choreography to showcase skills that Misty had honed in the studio. Misty wore a simple black leotard, a pink chiffon skirt, and a rose in her hair. It was the first time she performed a ballet solo, and she was smitten by the experience.

The Comfort of Structure

In ballet, Misty found structure. She found a way to reach for perfection. The teacher would give instruction, and she had the freedom to control the execution of the movement. It gave her a sense of power, control, and artistry that she'd never known, and it was a sharp contrast to what was happening at home. Ballet got her through the day, and she continued her lessons at the ballet studio for three years. But it was not easy. Bradley gave her a ride to the studio every afternoon, and Misty caught the bus for the one-hour ride home to the motel. The back and forth to and from the ballet studio took a toll on Misty. It was also affecting her big sister, Erica, who often rode the bus to get Misty from class and bring her home. It was exhausting for both girls, and DelaCerna wanted them to enjoy more time with friends and family. She told Misty that she'd have to quit ballet. But Misty protested. She lived for ballet. It was hers. It was what made her unique. When Misty broke the news to Bradley, the teacher invited the young dancer to live with her and her family in a condo across town. Bradley's idea was not new. Plenty of aspiring students and athletes have lived with teachers and coaches in order to focus on their training. Considering the family's circumstances, DelaCerna agreed.

Bradley's family accepted Misty without reservation. Their home life was structured, peaceful, and comforting for Misty. She shared a room with their three-year-old son, Wolf. Misty was included in family life. She walked Misha, their poodle, which was named after one of the

Mikhail Baryshnikov

Mikhail "Misha" Baryshnikov was born in Latvia, then a part of the communist Soviet Union. He began his ballet training at age nine and worked his way up in the Kirov Ballet to become a principal dancer in 1969. In 1974, he defected to Canada, longing for more personal and professional freedom. He danced with major ballet companies, including the New York City Ballet as a principal dancer. It was with NYCB that he worked with George Balanchine and Jerome Robbins.[13]

From 1980–1990, Baryshnikov served as ABT's artistic director. He went on to cofound the White Oak Dance Project with choreographer Mark Morris. White Oak expanded the repertoire and visibility of American modern dance. Baryshnikov directed and danced in the company from 1990 to 2002. In 2005, he established the Baryshnikov Arts Center in New York City. About 500 artists from all disciplines gather in this venue to create and present their work. Its arts education program exposes local high school students to contemporary performance and skills for a career in the arts.[14]

During his lifetime of professional work, Baryshnikov has won world recognition for his classical and contemporary range on stage, creative intuition behind the scenes, and mission to expand the world's appreciation of dance.

greatest ballet dancers of the twentieth century, Mikhail Baryshnikov.

Misty life with the Bradleys focused on three things: school, dance, and family time. She endeared herself to Bradley's parents, Bubby and Papa, and would join them at synagogue. Misty was the only person of color in the congregation. Bubby used this as a teaching moment. They watched the 1967 film *To Sir, with Love,* which tells the story of an African American teacher who mentors a class of mostly white troublemakers in a London school. Bubby pointed out that the film's star, Sidney Poitier, had broken racial barriers as the first black man to win an Oscar for his performance in another movie, *Lilies of the Field* (1963). Bubby believed that Misty was like Poitier, breaking through barriers in ballet.

A New Dream

Misty's interest in the drill team began to wane. Her coach, Liz Cantine, understood. She knew Misty was destined for ballet. It was the young girl's new dream. Cantine and her husband teamed up with Bradley to financially support the aspiring dancer. Bradley offered a full scholarship and rides, while the Cantines paid for expensive pointe shoes, tights, and leotards. The Cantines considered themselves to be Misty's honorary godparents, and their financial support and presence at her performances continued for years later. They continue to be a part of Copeland's support circle today.

It didn't take long for Bradley and Cantine to start calling Misty a prodigy. A prodigy is a child that has an amazing gift or talent for their young age. The

25

ladies knew that Misty would be a big name in ballet one day, and since professional careers for dancers start early and do not last a lifetime, Misty had to put in the work now and receive as much help as possible in order to reach her potential. Technique classes were always a part of her lessons, but dining etiquette, cultural know-how, and connecting with the African American dance community also supplemented her training. The Bradleys worked with Misty to help her come out of her shell and find her voice. They encouraged her to wear her hair naturally and eat healthy food

to sustain her body during the demanding ballet curriculum. At age fifteen, Misty was homeschooled, which allowed her to concentrate solely on her training.

When *The Nutcracker* premiered in Russia in December 1892, it was not well received. In 1954, George Balanchine re-created the ballet. Today, *The Nutcracker* is one of the world's most beloved classical ballets, and Clara is a coveted role for ballerinas.

Becoming "Clara"

In addition to the classes she took each day, Misty attended a pas de deux class to learn how to dance with a partner. Her partner lifted, twirled, and tossed her, which helped her dance the role of "Clara" in *The Nutcracker*. This classic story tells the tale of a young girl whose holiday present, a toy nutcracker, magically comes to life on Christmas Eve. Misty's performance was performed at the San Pedro High School. Her friends and family were in attendance and were so proud of her performance.

At fourteen, Misty danced the lead in another *Nutcracker*-style ballet, this time as "Clare" in Debbie Allen's *The Chocolate Nutcracker*. It was a variation on the classic story, performed by members of the African American dance community. Misty's "Clare" traveled the world, learning ethnic dance forms. For example, she performed African and Brazilian dance movements to live drumming—all while wearing pointe shoes! Misty spent hours working privately with choreographers to be certain she was well trained for the role. Performances were held all over Los Angeles. Her proud mother was in the front row. Misty received standing ovations and was later praised by Debbie Allen as a "child who dances in her soul."[15] Local newspapers ran her story, and fans even called the San Pedro Dance Center asking for Misty's next schedule of performances. Through this experience, Misty was able to meet prominent African Americans. She got a taste for what it means to stay connected to the community and to support one another.

CHAPTER THREE

A Dream in the Making

· ·

While she was living with the Bradleys, Misty discovered the American Ballet Theatre (ABT). It is the nation's most prestigious ballet company. Much like she did with the video of Nadia Comaneci, Misty watched ABT on a videotape for hours, eventually wearing it out. Company legends—Gelsey Kirkland, Rudolf Nureyev, Natalia Makarova, and Paloma Herrera—became her heroes.[1]

American Ballet Theatre

ABT is as one of the world's most prestigious dance companies. It was founded in 1940 with the goal of developing a well-rounded repertoire of classical ballets and new works from talented modern-day choreographers. ABT's dancers—from corps members to soloists and principals—tour the United States and international countries presenting its extensive repertoire. Included are nineteenth-century ballets (*Giselle, Sleeping Beauty,* and *Swan Lake*), twentieth-century ballets (*Apollo, Jardin aux Lilas, Les Sylphides,*

Misty Copeland and ABT's artistic director Kevin McKenzie participate in a panel to celebrate the ballet company's seventy-fifth anniversary. ABT is known as one of the world's premier dance companies for its work both on and off stage.

and *Rodeo*), and contemporary pieces (*Airs, Duets,* and *Push Comes to Shove*). ABT also presents commissioned works by master choreographers, such as George Balanchine, Agnes de Mille, Jerome Robbins, Twyla Tharp, and Antony Tudor. Former ABT principal dancer Kevin McKenzie has served as artistic director since 1992. He works to preserve the company's traditions while championing new dance innovations.[2]

Hero Worship

While watching ABT on video, Misty studied the technique of her heroes. She mimicked what they did with their heads and arms, how they moved their wrists and elbows, and how their feet performed the intricate footwork. She also applied this newfound knowledge to her own dancing. Bradley had also been honing Misty's musicality, which often falls second to placement and strength in classical training. Musicality would later give Misty an edge over other dancers, as she masterfully blended it with movement and performance.

During that time, Misty was also introduced to Balanchine's classical ballet *Don Quixote.* A video of the performance captured the pas de deux performed by Mikhail Baryshnikov and Gelsey Kirkland. Kirkland had been a famous ballerina in the 1960s and 1970s.[4] She was one of George Balanchine's muses, and she inspired the revival of his *Firebird* ballet.[5] In *Don Quixote*, Kirkland danced the lead role of Kitri,

> **"On April 27, 2006, an act of Congress made ABT America's National Ballet Company."**[3]

the innkeeper's daughter. She was strong and spunky, refusing to marry a wealthy noble and preferring a barber. At the end of the pas de deux, Kitri refuses her partner's hand in fierce independence only to balance on her own. Inspired, Misty longed to someday dance the role herself.[6]

Following in Herrera's Footsteps

Misty got to see the role performed live at Dorothy Chandler Pavilion in Los Angeles. Paloma Herrera, ABT's new principal dancer from Buenos Aires, Argentina, was dancing the role of Kitri. The role of

Paloma Herrera was only nineteen when she became an ABT principal dancer—one of the youngest in the company. Herrera is known for her musicality, commitment, articulate feet, and passion for ballet.

Paloma Herrera

As an aspiring dancer, Paloma Herrera won South American competitions, studied in Russia, and was a finalist at the Fourteenth International Ballet Competition in Varna, Bulgaria. ABT's Natalia Makarova invited the young dancer to study in London with the English National Ballet. Herrera was also encouraged to study at the School of American Ballet in New York. There she was chosen to dance a lead role at the annual performance. In 1991, she became a member of ABT's corps de ballet. Two years later, she became a soloist. Then in 1995, as a nineteen-year-old, she competed against older, more experienced dancers to become a principal dancer.[7]

Basilio was danced by Angel Corella. The two Latinos made a perfect duo, and Misty was on the edge of her seat for the entire show. She wanted even more to be up there one day, to dance as Kitri.[8]

Misty pored over newspapers and dance magazines that highlighted Paloma Herrera. She admired the advertisements in which Herrera appeared. Misty also dreamed of following in the dancer's footsteps, of performing with a major company as soon as possible, and of becoming a soloist or principal dancer. But self-doubt set in. She was worried that she'd started too late. And just like that, Misty talked herself out of these aspirations. Fast-forward four years later, and a seventeen-year-old Misty would meet her idol.[9]

Los Angeles Music Center's Spotlight Awards

Misty continued to work hard in her classes and at her many performances. She had been studying ballet for two years when Bradley gave her dream role—Kitri. The San Pedro Dance Center was set to perform the ballet *Don Quixote*. While preparing for the performance, Bradley encouraged Misty to enter the prestigious Music Center's Spotlight Awards in 1997 in Los Angeles. Notable judges were in attendance, including Gerald Arpino. He was the cofounder and artistic director of the Joffrey Ballet.

Misty was to perform a demanding variation from *Don Quixote*, one that ended with 32 *fouetté rond de jambe en tournants*. These turns are very difficult, requiring the dancer to balance on one leg while the second leg whips around. Fouettés are performed in succession, which can be tricky if the dancer does not have the strength or stamina to make the last turn as good as the first.

The competition aired on a local television station. Not only was Misty competing, but she was also featured on the program *Beating the Odds*. It followed select competitors at auditions, at rehearsals, and at home. Misty rehearsed six days a week for about one month in preparation for this competition.

The competition was intense, and the fifteen-year-old's nerves were getting the best of her. There was so much pressure. The public was watching, and she was exhausted. Bradley was concerned and decided to shake things up in a way that would ease her student's stress. She took Misty to the underground garage and put a copy of Misty's music in the cassette player of her car.

She calmed Misty by telling her that the judges would not focus on the turns but rather on her passion and potential. Bradley then reworked the ending. Instead of 32 fouettés, Misty would perform 16, followed by a pique manèges. These traveling turns are less demanding. Their "pricked" quality is performed on one leg in a circle on the stage. Once on stage, Misty performed with amazing passion. She wore a red costume embellished in gold lace, a costume that Bradley had made, and executed every move to perfection.

From this experience, Misty learned the importance of having of a backup plan. This signified true professionalism. It was a triumphant moment for the dancer, as she received a trophy—which is in her home today—and $5,000 for ballet training.

Misty's mother, Lindsey, Bradley, and Bubby were in the audience, clapping and cheering. Gerald Arpino, too, loved her performance so much that he immediately invited her to the Joffery Ballet's summer dance intensive![10]

Auditions and Introductions

Misty's next step was to audition for a summer dance intensive put on by a top ballet company. Dance intensives give young dancers the opportunity to train and network with elite instructors. She'd already been invited to the Joffrey's intensive. Plus, she'd been approached by ABT's summer intensive director, Rebecca Wright, also a judge at the Music Center's Spotlight Awards. But Misty wasn't automatically "in" at either intensive. She still had to audition to determine the size of the scholarship they'd offer. Misty also auditioned for Dance Theatre of Harlem, New York City Ballet, Pacific NW Ballet, and the San Francisco Ballet Company. Every company offered her scholarships, with the exception of the NYCB. They sent her a rejection letter. Bradley believed that the rejection was solely based on Misty's skin color. Misty decided upon the San Francisco Ballet. It was close to home and offered enough scholarship money to cover airfare, tuition, and room and board.[11]

In June 1998, Misty headed off to San Francisco. It was the first time she had been on her own, and the second time she'd been on a plane. The year prior, she'd flown to South Dakota. Charles Maple, former ABT soloist and studio partner, had invited her to travel with him to perform as a guest dancer in a revised *The Nutcracker*. Maple and Misty had prepared for months, and she'd already learned the choreography. However, when she took the audition with about one hundred female dancers—all of whom were white—Maple asked that she pretend the choreography was new to her. Misty was hurt and confused, but she complied. Maple later explained that he wanted her to be Clara, but the other dancers and their parents needed to see that her casting was due to talent, not to any special feelings about her color. They did see that, and they were very welcoming and appreciative of her obvious ability. Misty danced as Clara in two performances.[12]

Summer Intensity

At the summer dance intensive, Misty shared the experience with about two hundred other students, approximately eighty males and the rest females. She worked hard and made friends with dancers of various ethnicities. After the placement class, she was placed in the highest-level classes. Not only did she have the ideal ballet body, but she had the movement quality that could handle the advanced material. When not in class, she and her friends toured the city.

Despite her natural talent, Misty had a lot of catching up to do. She needed to learn the steps, their French names, and even the ballets her peers had been performing for years. Misty learned by watching the other dancers. She listened and imitated, following along. If she didn't know something, her teacher would pull her aside to show her. Misty also lacked the stamina needed for such an intense schedule. Dancing en pointe for hours left her feet red and swollen. Long days were finished with her feet in trash cans that had been morphed into ice buckets. But with all of that, she still shined among her peers. Plus, she was used to demonstrate partnering in her pas de deux classes.

At the end of the intensive, the San Francisco Ballet Company extended a special invitation to Misty. They wanted her to study with them for the full year. It was an honor that only a small handful of students were given. Although appreciative, Misty decided to pass. Her mother wanted her home with the family, and Bradley wanted to continue her training. Plus, Misty's dream was still ABT. She intended to attend their summer intensive in New York City the following summer.[13]

Tug-of-War

DelaCerna repeatedly told Misty that she'd like to have her home again after the summer dance intensive in San

Francisco. Misty had changed so much, in the way she carried herself and with food choices. DelaCerna thought Bradley had brainwashed her and was using the dancer to promote the San Pedro Dance Center. DelaCerna also worried that she was losing her daughter, much like she had lost so many others in her life. Bradley, on the other hand, wanted Misty to resume living with her and training at the San Pedro Dance Center. She knew the young dancer had holes in her training and wanted to help her prepare for her future career.

It took Misty some time to wrap her young mind—and later her adult mind—around this emotional tug-of-war. She knew that Bradley's goal was to open her heart and home, giving the aspiring dancer a place to develop. At the same time, she began to feel that she had outgrown the San Pedro Dance Center and was ready for the next stage in her training. And yet, it was in the Bradley's home that Misty realized she deserved more out of life than what her mother had provided. The Bradleys loved her and taught her how to find her voice. And although DelaCerna loved Misty fiercely, she and Misty's siblings couldn't understand the significance of the professional opportunities that awaited.[14]

DelaCerna and Bradley's relationship waned. Cantine helped DelaCerna locate the Lauridsen Ballet Centre in Torrence, California. Misty thought life as she knew it would be over if she moved on without Bradley. DelaCerna called Bradley and informed her that Misty could attend class the next evening at the San Pedro Dance Center, but afterward, Bradley was to drive her home to the motel. On the way to the motel, Bradley

Misty Copeland is photographed at the Lauridsen Ballet Centre in 1998. She trained hard, knowing that the longevity of dancer's career is shorter than that of other professionals. Copeland credits ballet for teaching her commitment, discipline, and sacrifice.

explained the concept of legal emancipation. Others like Misty had pursued this legal action too, desiring the opportunity to make their own decisions about their lives and careers. Bradley and Misty drove to a nearby coffee shop and met with a lawyer. He explained how the emancipation worked. Misty would have to petition the court to be declared an emancipated minor.

A National Headline

Although she didn't want to hurt anyone, Misty decided to pursue emancipation. Instead of going to the motel, Misty stayed with a friend from the studio. The lawyer contacted her mother. In turn, DelaCerna called the police and the media. Misty stayed at her friend's house for three days before the lawyer and two police officers came to the door. They were there to take her to the police station, where she met her mother. Misty was in tears on the way home to the motel. She was angry. She thought her mother was selfish and that her training was over. Misty retreated from everything and everyone. She shares in her memoir, *Life in Motion: An Unlikely Ballerina*, that leaving was the most difficult thing she had to do. It was more distressing than any of the other moves she had experienced as a child.

DelaCerna took the Bradleys to court. She claimed that they manipulated her daughter into filing for emancipation and wanted to file a restraining order to keep them away from the dancer. The national media latched on to the story, and the Bradleys tried to set the record straight in court and with the press. Things eventually began to settle down, and Misty withdrew her emancipation petition. The Bradleys stayed away, and the restraining order request naturally fell away.

The Next Chapter

Sixteen-year-old Misty enrolled in the eleventh grade at San Pedro High School. Everyone at school knew what had been happening, and producers even offered to do a television show or feature film of her story. She was mortified, but she thought of her idol, Paloma Herrera, in the role of the fiercely independent Kitri. Misty decided to muster up the courage to be strong and get through the situation. She threw herself back into ballet, polishing her technique at the new studio, Lauridsen Ballet Centre. Her new classmates embraced her, especially Kaylen Ratto and Ashley Ellis. The girls were inseparable, and their friendship helped to heal Misty's heart.

Although Misty was moving on, the drama wasn't over between DelaCerna and Bradley. They appeared on a talk show called *Leeza*. DelaCerna wanted public support, while Bradley wanted to set the record straight. Fellow San Pedro Dance Center students were in the audience, pleading that Misty return. Misty, who didn't want to be there, sat in the audience with her siblings. She didn't want any of the attention and was especially mortified when the host, Leeza Gibbons, began asking her questions.[15] Her classmates had tuned in at school, and Misty felt so exposed. But there was nothing more to do than to keep pressing on. Slowly things were looking up. Her mother got a job, and the family moved into a two-bedroom apartment. DelaCerna was taking care of the family again, this time without leaning on a man. Misty appreciated her mother once again.

CHAPTER FOUR

Taking Her Place on Stage

• • • • • • • • • • • • •

True to her word, Misty Copeland auditioned for ABT's dance intensive in 1999. She was offered a full scholarship and arrived in New York City that June. The sixteen-year-old stayed in a convent in Greenwich Village. Other dance intensive students—both at ABT and at other companies—stayed at the convent too. This included Misty's friends, Kaylen Ratto (studying at the Joffrey intensive) and Ashley Ellis (at the ABT intensive). Misty worked hard that summer, and she was told that ABT planned to invite her to join their Studio Company. She was ecstatic.[1]

At the year-end recital, Misty was slotted to perform a contemporary pas de deux and a principal variation from the classical ballet *Paquita*. The lead character is a Spanish gypsy, Paquita, who saves the life of a French aristocrat only to learn that she is also nobility. After the show, Misty received the anticipated invitation for the Studio Company. It was a training program for promising dancers, which after a certain period of time would lead to an invitation to the main company. Misty was beside herself and told them she needed to ask her mother. Misty raced to the convent to call her mother with the news. DelaCerna surprised her by saying the decision was up to her.

Misty weighed the pros and cons. She still had one more year of high school, and she knew she wasn't ready to be in New York on her own. Plus, her sister Erica was having a baby. Misty wanted to be home to welcome her new niece, named after Mariah Carey, into the world. She ultimately decided to postpone until the next year.

ABT understood and offered her the Coca-Cola Scholarship to cover the cost of her shoes and training. She was also guaranteed a spot with the Studio Company after her graduation in 2000.

> **"At ABT's summer intensive, Misty met Paloma Herrera. The two later became friends."** [2]

During her senior year, Misty not only trained but did what other teens her age did. She hung out with friends and went to the prom. But once her diploma was in hand, Misty boarded the plane for her new home—New York City and ABT. [3]

An ABT Identity

Once again, Copeland was in ABT's summer dance intensive. Only this time, she was more invested as a member of the ABT organization. Misty moved in to a brownstone on Manhattan's Upper West Side with former ABT dancers Isabel and Kelly Brown. Misty studied classical ballet, as well as contemporary dance. ABT appreciated her range and ability to successfully perform both styles.

Joining Misty at the intensive was her good friend Ashley Ellis. In the year-end performance, both teenagers were offered leading roles. When the intensive drew to a close, Kevin McKenzie informed Misty that he wanted her to apprentice with the main company before joining the Studio Company. This meant that she'd get to join them for a performance tour in China. It would be her first international trip. On a limited contract, she danced behind the soloists and principal dancers as a member of the corps de ballet. It was a great honor, especially since she lacked professional experience.

Upon her return in 2000, Copeland was made an official member of ABT's Studio Company. Joining her were five other females and six males—all of whom where preparing to join ABT's main company. They traveled and performed in the United States and in Bermuda. They also

Ashley Ellis is a principal dancer for the Boston Ballet in Massachusetts. She began training at age six. Ellis met Misty Copeland as a student at Lauridsen Ballet Centre.

addressed young audience members in question-and-answer sessions after the performances. Copeland felt at home in the Studio Company, and she was developing her identity as an ABT ballerina. She also built strong friendships with female dancers of mixed ethnicities.[4]

Stepping into the Corps de Ballet

In 2001, the nineteen-year-old Copeland joined ABT's corps de ballet.[5] It was part of the main company, and it consisted of about fifty dancers. About twelve soloists and twenty principal dancers rounded out the company. ABT has two performance seasons, one in the fall for three to four weeks, and one in the spring for eight weeks. Both take place in New York City. This schedule is supplemented with classes, rehearsals, and national and international touring. All in all, ABT dancers work thirty-five weeks a year. Classes and rehearsals run Tuesday through Sunday. They also take a two-month break, also known as "layoffs," in the summer. This free time allows company members to take advantage of new dance opportunities, all the while continuing to keep their bodies in tip-top shape.

The corps de ballet is very competitive. Dancers are determined to make their mark, eager to catch the attention of company directors. They hope to stand out for a featured role or promotion. ABT does not audition its dancers. Rather, Kevin McKenzie and the choreographers observe class and performances, deciding how to cast upcoming performances and who to promote. It was in the corps that Copeland realized that her natural talents and past achievements were no longer enough to help her achieve her goals. She had to work hard, keep training, continue growing, and pace herself through long, intense schedules. During her layoffs, even today, Copeland takes ballet classes, as well as Pilates and cardio classes, to keep up her skills and physical agility.[6]

Uncomfortable in Her Own Skin

ABT dancers have a grueling schedule, especially during performance season. Copeland threw herself in her work, until she experienced agonizing pain in her lower back during one late night rehearsal. Copeland kept dancing and finally went to a doctor for an MRI two weeks later. The diagnosis revealed that Copeland had a stress fracture in her lower lumbar vertebrae. It had been an injury in the making for the past year. Copeland was forced to turn down *The Nutcracker*'s Clara, the coveted role she had been given. The recovery process lasted a year: six months in a backbrace, and six months in rehabilitation to regain strength and flexibility.

Back at ABT, Copeland went to her doctor for a routine physical. Her doctor was concerned that the nineteen-year-old weighed less than 100 pounds (45 kilograms) and had not yet menstruated. This could affect bone strength.[7] The decision was made to induce late-onset puberty.[8]

During the next few weeks, her body changed. She menstruated, gained 10 pounds (4.5 kilograms), and developed her feminine curves. She felt awkward in her new body, and now her skin color was not the only thing that set her apart from her counterparts—at least in appearance.[9] She had lost her petite frame, which was unacceptable in the world of ballet. Copeland couldn't dance like she used to, and it was almost like she had to start all over again. She felt uncomfortable, even lost.[10] Even sharing costumes in the corps, which is common, was tough now that she was more curvacious than her fellow dancers. Copeland was embarrassed, and her confidence wavered.[11]

Adjustments and Acceptance

ABT directors told her to "lengthen," even at five foot two inches and topping over 100 pounds. It was a soft and not-so-subtle way of saying, "lose some weight."[12] They encouraged her to regain her classical line, but Copeland rebelled. She ate high fat foods to soothe herself, which included entire boxes of Krispy Kreme doughnuts. But junk food made things worse. She gained weight and felt terrible in class.

Copeland realized that she needed to eat healthy foods, as well as increase cardio workouts to keep from bulking up her muscles. It took five years to really know her body and what it needed to perform well. Copeland omitted white sugar, flour, and salt from her diet. She also took a Pilates class for core-strenthening. Copeland skipped out on chicken, beef, and pork, and instead opted for seafood. ABT noticed the changes and eventually accepted her curves and musculature as a part of who she was as a dancer.

On Her Own

Copeland later moved into her own place. It was an apartment she affectionately called "the dungeon." Its only windows were barred, and it faced the building next door with only five inches in between. And even

Copeland struggled in her early years as a dancer because her body simply wasn't like the traditional ballerina body. She was muscular and curvy, and she was often told she'd never make it.

thought it had roaches, it was all hers. When not in class or at home, Copeland explored the city. Broadway shows, street fairs, art galleries—she loved it all. She especially loved going dancing at nightclubs. One night, accompanied by a friend, Copeland went to Lotus, a popular destination for professionals and celebrities. There, she met her future first boyfriend-turned-husband, Olu Evans. They were introduced by Evans's cousin, the actor Taye Diggs.

The two hit it off. Like Copeland, Evans was of mixed ethnicity. His mother was Jewish, and his father was African American. Evans lived in Atlanta and studied law at Emory Law School. Copeland and Evans had a long distance relationship until he eventually moved to New York City. Copeland had a

> **"Copeland learned that if she was good to her body, it would be good to her."**

great deal of respect for Evans, crediting him for helping her to find her voice. Evans encouraged her to go to McKenzie, to tell him that she wanted to be a ballerina, to dance classical roles, not just contemporary works. When she finally did it, McKenzie agreed with what she had to say. She could dance both. That was it. And then McKenzie gave her the space in which to back up her wishes with actions.

Black Swans

On May 6, 2007, the *New York Times* published "Where Are All the Black Swans?" by Gia Kourlas. It was a

Blending In and Standing Out

Ballet is European, which means that it is considered to be a "white" art form. Its stories tell of magical creatures from other worlds, such as swans and ghosts. Ballet dancers are expected to blend with one other in height, weight, technique, and even skin color. This is especially true for "white ballets," such as *Giselle*, *Swan Lake*, and *La Bayadère*. If dancers of color were cast in the corps, they sometimes had to apply white powder to their faces to blend in. Raven Wilkinson, the 1950's dancer who later mentored Copeland, had to do this, too. Misty even faced this when cast in the role of *Sleeping Beauty's* Puss in Boots. She questioned the reasoning behind the cat having to be white. Instead, she wanted to be a brown cat and took the stage as such.

powerful article that stirred a great deal of emotions for Copeland. It pointed out that in 1933, Lincoln Kirstein dreamed of remaking ballet for America and implementing diversity among ballet students. His plan was to bring in sixteen teenage dancers—evenly split between male and female, and black and white. However, the diversity Kirstein wanted took longer than expected.

Although dancers of various ethnicities dance classical ballet, inequality continues, especially for African American women. Male dancers on the other hand, have enjoyed some success. One in particular was Arthur Mitchell. Mitchell had been a principal dancer for the New York City Ballet before founding the world-renowned Dance Theatre of Harlem in 1969.

Kourlas's article also discussed the directors/choreographers who promote diverse dancers and the difficulties of getting hired by major companies. Kourlas writes, "On a deeper level many black dancers suggest that a primary obstacle is stereotyping. Black women are perceived as being forceful, which doesn't square with the ethereal image of a ballerina." She quotes Raven Wilkinson as saying, "I have wondered if women have a harder time because ballet, as Balanchine said, is woman. That purity, that sense of leaving the earth and the romantic sense of being on point is the idea of the woman on the pedestal. Whereas the black woman is seen as more earthy and as dancing solidly." Kourlas also highlighted the lack of black students coming up through the ranks, much like Copeland was doing at the time. Virginia Johnson, former Dance Theatre of Harlem dancer and *Pointe* magazine editor, believes this is because of "artistic vision, economics—ballet is expensive and competitive among women no matter their skin color—and culture," as noted by Kourlas. Johnson points out that being the only black dancer is challenging, and she further states:

> You feel separate, and you feel negated in a certain sense, and it's not that people are trying to make you feel bad, but it's just obviously around you. Everyone else can bond by similarity, and you have to make an effort, and making an effort makes you wonder, "Am I not being true to myself?" It's hard to

Copeland is passionate about changing the face of ballet. She wants it to reflect the diversity of the American public. Copeland takes opportunities to share the beauty of the art form with kids who may not have access to it.

be strong enough to be in that environment and to not feel wrong.

Kourlas's article challenged ballet companies to diversify by going into non-dance communities to expose would-be dancers to the art form and train them, if possible. It also touched on the importance of role models—accomplished dancers mentoring aspiring dancers. Role models show that dreams of dancing are possible, and despite the difficulty of the journey, these dreams make the destination so worth it.[13]

For Copeland, "Where Are All the Black Swans?" articulated the loneliness she had felt for six years in the corps. She was angry, sad, and without anyone in the company to relate or understand. There simply weren't any other African American women in the company. Fellow dancers, thinking they were empathetic, would say they didn't think of her as black. But this wasn't helpful. Then she wasn't always considered for classical roles, not because of talent but because of her skin color. Then there were those in the audience and on social media who were critical, not wanting to lose the traditional image of a white ballerina.

There are only a few African American women in major ballet companies. "They are being told they won't fit in, they won't have a successful career, they don't have the bodies. Even to this day, I hear that I shouldn't even be wearing a tutu, I don't have the right legs, my muscles are too big," Copeland says. She admits that there are those times when she questions herself. "Because to me I think I look like a ballerina, and I feel like a ballerina, but maybe I'm not seeing what other people are seeing." But she forged ahead, thanks to the help of others.[14]

Friends, Mentors, and Patrons

Copeland often felt alone as a black swan in a white swan world. She was still pushing herself to achieve her ABT goal, but she had considered leaving to dance with other companies, such as NYCB or Dance Theatre of Harlem. She also looked to other African American females for friendship and inspiration. Victoria Rowell, a ballerina-turned-actor, showed Copeland what it meant to be a successful African Americn woman in Hollywood. Susan Fales-Hill, a Harvard graduate, author, socialite, and a member of ABT's board of trustees, encouraged the dancer to press through when she thought about giving up. Fales-Hill shared kind words, wisdom, and hope, and eventually sponsored Copeland as a patron.

Raven Wilkinson and Misty Copeland attend a screening of the documentary *A Ballerina's Tale* in 2015. Wilkinson, a former ballet dancer, has been a trailblazer for African American dancers. She is also a mentor to Copeland.

Copeland also discovered Raven Wilkinson while watching a documentary on Ballet Russe de Monte Carlo. In the mid-1950s, Wilkinson had become one of the first African American ballerinas to dance with a major ballet company. She was on the full-time roster of the Ballet Russe de Monte Carlo. While on tour in the United State, the company went to the Deep South and experienced blatant racism from the Ku Klux Klan. In 1961, Wilkinson quit Ballet Russe and later became a dancer for the Dutch National Ballet in the Netherlands. She returned to the United States in 1973 and danced and acted for the New York City Opera until 2011.[15]

Copeland felt a kinship to Wilkinson and learned that the former ballerina also lived in New York City. Arrangements were made for the two to meet for a public conversation at a Studio Museum event in Harlem. Wilkinson, who had been a long-time fan, became a mentor and often attended Copeland's performances. Copeland felt a responsibility to share Wilkinson's story, as well as those of other black dancers who made significant contributions to ballet.

CHAPTER FIVE

Representing the American Dancer

• •

In 2007, ABT artistic director Kevin McKenzie nominated Misty Copeland, along with fellow corps dancer Jared Matthews, to represent ABT at the very prestigious Erik Bruhn competition in Canada. Prizes were awarded to two dancers—one male and one female—with top technical ability and artistic achievement.[1] Four of the world's best ballet companies were represented: ABT, the Royal Ballet, the Royal Danish Ballet, and the National Ballet of Canada. Each company selected two dancers. Copeland planned to bring a grand pas de deux from *Sleeping Beauty*, a contemporary piece, and an excerpt from Jirí Kylián's *Petite Mort*. Three days before the competition, she developed a stress reaction in her metatarsal. Although she went on with the performance, Copeland and Matthews did not win. And yet, Copeland was well on her to way to winning much more.[2]

A Loss Leads to a "Solo" Achievement

A few weeks after the Erik Bruhn competition in August 2007, McKenzie invited Copeland to become an ABT soloist. He had seen her as a true ballerina during the competition and believed that she was ready for the role. It was an exhilarating moment for the twenty-four-year-old. She was grateful for McKenzie's support and guidance, and she knew that her achievement could further inspire black women in ballet. Copeland's promotion made her the second African American female soloist with ABT,

The History of Ballet

Fifteenth-century Italian Renaissance nobility used ballet in court celebrations. In the sixteenth century, ballet made it to the French court. In the seventeenth century, King Louis XIV of France transformed ballet into a true art form. Ballet moved from court to the stage, at first with operas, and by the mid-1700s, on its own. Early nineteenth-century ballets told of spirits and magic. Ballerinas wore romantic tutus and performed en pointe. Ballet reached new heights in Russia in the second half of the nineteenth century. Technique was more challenging, with turnout, high leg extensions, leaps, and turns. Ballerinas then wore a shorter, stiffer classical tutu to show leg lines and footwork.

In the early twentieth century, Russian choreographers experimented beyond classical technique and costuming, and George Balanchine expanded the classical form even further. His neo-classical ballets were more contemporary, favoring musicality and human emotion. Today, ballet offers classical storytelling and contemporary expressiveness.[3]

and the company's first in twenty years. She was also one of the youngest ABT dancers to experience such a promotion.[4]

In 2008, Misty Copeland was honored with the Leonore Annenberg Fellowship in the Arts.[5] It awarded "$50,000 a year for up to two years to talented young artists to broaden their skills and make a breakthrough in their industry."[6] Copeland decided to invest in private lessons with Merrill Ashley[7], a former NYCB principal and Balanchine expert who stages his ballets for companies around the world.[8] "I felt that a lot of the Balanchine ballets were my weakness," Copeland says. "I need to learn quick foot work and still stay open and free on top."[9] Her investment afforded her more opportunities to dance classical roles, which had been a long-time goal.

As a soloist, Copeland danced all sorts of roles and styles. And while she performed in contemporary pieces from Twyla Tharp and Paul Taylor's Company B, it was her classical pieces that really stood out. *Dance Magazine*'s Astrida Woods wrote the following on September 10, 2012:

> But it's her classical repertoire that has deepened in artistry with each season. In the peasant pas de deux from Giselle, she is buoyant and refreshingly lyrical, and her plush jumps in Swan Lake's pas de trois are a joy. As the Fairy of Valor in *Sleeping Beauty*, she tempers the harsh stabbing fingers and dagger-like pas de chats by uplifting her body with grandeur and, yes, valor.

Copeland performs some of the most challenging roles in classical ballet. She puts in many rehearsal hours to make the unnatural movements of ballet look effortless, as demonstrated in ABT's *Giselle* at the Metropolitan Opera House in May 2015.

Woods quotes Kevin McKenzie as saying, "Misty is enormously versatile. She knows how to listen, realize and apply. She is a real representation of the American dancer. I obviously believe in Misty. She has earned everything she has achieved."[10]

Rave Reviews 2012

Also in 2012, Copeland performed the role of Gamzatti in *La Bayadère*. This ballet, originally choreographed by Marius Petipa, is set in Royal India. It centers around a love triangle among Nikiya, an enticing temple dancer (*bayadère*), the scheming Gamzatti, and Solor the warrior. The Huffington Post's Margaret Fuhrer wrote the following in her May 29, 2012, review:

So when a young ABT soloist does get a Giselle or a Juliet, it's a big deal. These dancers aren't dropped, fully formed, in front of us. We've watched them grow up at ABT—spotted them in the corps de ballet early on, tracked each of their hard-earned solos, speculated about when the promotion might come, kvelled when it did. They're our hometown heroes, and when they're given a chance to stand center stage, we root for them.

Fuhrer continues:

Copeland really knows how to command the stage. She has mastered Gamzatti's considerable technical challenges, but you don't see her thinking about them as she dances. Her Gamzatti is cunning and feline, more than a little desperate, always just about to erupt.[11]

Firebird

Misty Copeland's ultimate dream was of being an ABT principal dancer. This promotion would allow her to focus on principal roles, instead of dancing lots of other roles in a single ballet. In 2012, the soloist was offered the great honor of dancing the lead role in *Firebird*. It was to be her first lead at ABT, playing the very same character Gelsey Kirkland danced alongside Mikhail Baryshnikov.

The original choreography had been done by Mikhail Fokine for Ballets Russes in 1910, and it had been reworked over the years by other choreographers working with ABT.[12] This time, Alexei Ratmansky was adding his own artistic touch to the magical story of love versus evil. When McKenzie asked her to learn the part of the mystical Firebird, Copeland thought she'd be an understudy. If the lead dancer were unable to perform, she'd step into the role. She was honored to have been asked and threw herself into the extra rehearsals. The role itself was demanding with two solos and a pas de deux.

While learning the choreography, she was also involved in a workshop at Dance Theatre of Harlem. During a rehearsal break, she casually scrolled through Twitter and learned that she was to dance in the second cast! (The first cast role had gone to

In July 2016, Misty Copeland wowed audiences with her leading role in *Firebird*. It was one of the most important roles of her career. She danced with an injury, but audiences couldn't tell as she flew across the stage.

a guest principal visiting ABT.) This made her the first African American woman to dance the role for a major ballet company. Tears and congratulations were in abundance that day, especially from the Dance Theatre of Harlem dancers, who understood the significance of such a casting. Additional support came from her ABT family and the African American community.

Firebird premiered on tour on March 29, 2012, before the season at the Metropolitan Opera in New York City. They danced at the Segerstrom Center for the Arts in Costa Mesa, California. Copeland's family came to support her, and the musician Prince organized an intimate celebration for them all.

> **"Copeland has visual memory, the ability to immediately remember anything she sees."**

Bringing *Firebird* Home

Copeland was prepping for the *Firebird* premiere at the Met, but her body was telling her that it was too much. Long rehearsals exhausted the left shin on her turning leg. The pain was intense, and she modified her leaps and the intricate footwork. Even a few hours before the first show at the Met, she wasn't sure if she'd be able to take the stage because the pain was so overwhelming. But so many people came out to support her, particularly those in the African American community—many for the first time. They knew what it meant to have an African American woman dancing this role for ABT at the Metropolitan Opera House. She knew that she had to do this.

Becoming Prince's Muse

Through her friend Kaylen Ratto, the late musician Prince reached out to Copeland in 2009. He was remaking his popular "Crimson and Clover" song, and he wanted her to dance in the video. She was free to choreograph her dance. She wore a couture gown, purchased as a gift by Prince. He also invited her to do other performances from time to time, including on his European tour. In working with him, she learned about being a whole artist, a total professional, passionate for one's fans, feeding off of them as artists. It was something she brought with her during her career.

Prince called again in 2011. He flew her to his home in Minnesota for a photo shoot. He also had an idea for a collaboration. He wanted to do a US tour called "Welcome to America." He wanted her to choreograph "The Beautiful Ones." Opportunities like these helped Copeland fine-tune her ballet technique, expose audiences to ballet, and reach new levels of growth as an artist.[13]

With a mind-over-matter approach, she ignored the throbbing pain and took the stage. For ninety minutes, she morphed into the Firebird. Her adrenaline kicked in, and she felt no pain. This was her moment, and she was rewarded with flowers, cheers from the crowd, and a standing ovation.

Prince invited Misty Copeland to dance during his Welcome 2 America tour. The late musician admired Copeland's talent and musicality, and she credits him for helping her to develop as an artist.

● ● ● ● ● ● ● ● ● ● ● ● ● ● ● ● ● ● ● ●

From Fractures to Fabulous

In the days that followed *Firebird,* the pain in Copeland's shin flooded back. She had six stress fractures in her tibia—three of which were nearly full breaks. She needed corrective surgery or else she would risk breaking the shin completely. Several doctors even told her that she may never dance again. In June 2012, she pulled out of the ABT season and underwent major surgery. A metal plate was put in her leg, followed by seven months of intense physical therapy.

Copeland refused to give up and kept her goal of becoming a principal dancer in front of her. She never rested in her mind, dancing on the inside. She added a private floor barre class, masseuse and acupuncturist appointments, and a private Gyrotonics class. She knew this was a temporary setback but felt the pressure of keeping her place in the company and pleasing her fans. She went back too soon, and while her performance was good for what she had to endure, it wasn't up to her standards. It took a lot of hard work to regain herself, and a year later, Copeland returned to the stage. She embraced her role model status by writing a memoir, starring in the popular "I Will What I Want" commercial for Under Armour, and sharing ballet with communities.

A "Club Kid" with Heart

Despite her work as a professional dancer and her other endeavors, Misty Copeland is all about giving back. She works with charitable organizations, and in particular, she mentors youth in her area and around the world. She aims to bring more diversity to ballet by exposing youth to the art form. In 2011, Copeland joined twenty Boys & Girls Club alumni for "Great Futures Start Here," a public service announcement (PSA). Directed by Academy Award winner Ron Howard, the short video calls attention to those issues that affect's America's youth: childhood obesity, high school dropout rate, and violence. It then shows how Boys & Girls Clubs transform lives. Joining Copeland were national co-spokespersons, Jennifer Lopez and

Misty Copeland is a National Youth of the Year Ambassador for Boys & Girls Clubs of America. As a mentor, she helps youths reach their full potential. Copeland has her own mentors who help her continue to reach new heights in her profession.

•••••••••••••••••••••

Denzel Washington, as well as Jackie Joyner-Kersee, Sugar Ray Leonard, Ne-Yo, Shaquille O'Neal, and Kerry Washington.[14]

In May 2012, she was inducted into the Boys & Girls Club National Hall of Fame in San Diego.[15] She was joined by her mother, the Cantines, and the Bradleys—all the drama from so long ago had been forgiven. In June 2013, Copeland was named National Youth of the Year Ambassador for the Boys & Girls Clubs of America.

CHAPTER SIX

The Talent and Will to Open Doors

· ·

During Misty Copeland's career, her onstage dedication and offstage role modeling has won the admiration of many. During Black History Month in 2011, *Essence* named Copeland as one of its 37 Boundary-Breaking Black Women in Entertainment. In 2012, she was honored with the Breakthrough Leadership Award by the Council of Urban Professionals. The following year, she received the Young, Gifted & Black honor at the 2013 Black Girls Rock! Awards. She also received an honorary doctor of fine arts degree from the University of Hartford in November 2014 for her contributions to classical ballet and to the diversification of the art form.[1]

Joining the President's Council on Fitness, Sports, and Nutrition

In 2014, US president Barack Obama appointed Copeland to the President's Council on Fitness, Sports, and Nutrition. The council was established

Misty Copeland uses any opportunity to educate the public about ballet, diversity, and inclusion. One such discussion took place at the White House. Copeland joined US president Barack Obama and *Time*'s Maya Rhodan at the White House in March 2016.

in 1956 by President Dwight D. Eisenhower's administration. At that time it was called the President's Council on Youth Fitness, but Obama updated its name and mission. According to fitness.gov, the council now "engages, educates, and empowers all Americans to adopt a healthy lifestyle that includes regular physical activity and good nutrition."[2] While talking with Copeland and *Time's* Maya Rhodan in February 2016, Obama explained why Copeland was selected:

...[A]s a father of two daughters, seeing how images of strong, athletic, accomplished women carry over, and encouraging them in sports and dance and how they move physically, it turns out that every study shows that young girls who are involved in sports, dance, athletics

Project Plié

Also in 2014, Misty Copeland helped with the launch of ABT's Project Plié. The program aimed to represent America's diversity in the nation's ballet companies.[5] It partnered with twenty-seven Boys & Girls Clubs across the country, as well as professional ballet companies, to introduce ballet to youngsters. Master classes were taught, and teachers identified students with ballet potential. (It was very similar to Cynthia Bradley's work with her local Boys & Girls Club class.) Project Plié then facilitates a connection with the ABT Project Plié Partner Teachers, as well as community companies and schools. Project Plié was a huge success. In 2015, classes were offered at 43 Boys & Girls Clubs, 991 students participated, and 68 of those students were offered the opportunity to train full-time.[6] Rachel S. Moore, the former CEO of American Ballet Theatre, had this to say on ABT.org:

> In launching Project Plié, American Ballet Theatre aims to take an important step toward helping the classical ballet profession better reflect the multicultural and ethnic diversity of our country's population. This initiative can assist ballet students from diverse backgrounds in reaching their full potential by providing them with the support and

active engagement of teachers, mentors and current professional dancers. We sincerely believe that diversifying the art form at its training level will strengthen and broaden the pipeline of future artists and help ensure ballet's continued relevance in the twenty-first century.[7]

end up having more confidence generally. And across the board in everything that they do end up being more assertive, happier. So this is one of the reasons why having Misty on our Fitness Council has been so important.[3]

The President's Council on Fitness, Sports, and Nutrition is headed by two co-chairs: three-time Olympic gymnast Dominique Dawes and Super Bowl champion Drew Brees. Council members, appointed by the president, advise and include top professionals in medicine, fitness, sports, education, and the culinary arts. Grant Hill, Rachael Ray, Caitlin Cahow, and Donna Richardson are among those who serve on the council.[4]

Becoming a Swan

Another monumental achievement for Copeland came in the fall of 2014. She was invited to dance the dual roles of Odette/Odile in one of the most popular classical ballets, *Swan Lake*. The ballet centers on the

Copeland and Brooklyn Mack rehearse *Swan Lake* at the Kennedy Center in 2015. Copeland is encouraged by the change in ballet's audiences. She works as an advocate to introduce and include minorities and the underprivileged to the ballet in America.

• • • • • • • • • • • • • • • • • • • •

tale of immense beauty, evil spells, and self-sacrifice for love. This significant casting made Copeland the first African American woman to dance the lead role for ABT. Copeland repeated the role during ABT's spring season in June 2015, along with her debut as Juliet in *Romeo & Juliet*.[8] In its June 26, 2015, review, the *New York Times* declared:

> Let everyone know henceforth that an African-American ballerina has danced this exalted role with American Ballet Theater at the prestigious Metropolitan Opera House. Let everyone

know that other African-American dancers, Raven Wilkinson (who danced with the Ballet Russe de Monte Carlo in 1955-61) and Lauren Anderson (who, with the Houston Ballet, was the first African-American ballerina to become a principal of an American ballet company), brought her bouquets onstage. And let everyone know that her fellow dancers shared her applause with pride.[9]

Putting Pen to Paper

Copeland shares her life story in a *New York Times* bestselling memoir, *Life in Motion*. Cowritten with award-winning journalist Charisse Jones, it was published in March 2014. The BookPage review called it "engaging" and noted:

> [Copeland is] a poised, intelligent writer whose temperament—disciplined, determined, driven—gives the book a special spark.... In *Life in Motion*, she looks back on the past without bitterness or anger, only gratitude. Hers is an out-of-the-ordinary story about defying stereotypes, and she shares it in an inspiring narrative that's enlivened by her own grace and generous spirit.[10]

Copeland went on to collaborate with award-winning illustrator and author Christopher Myers on *Firebird* (2014), an inspirational book for children. It tells of a young girl who overcomes fear to achieve her goals.

Misty Copeland appears at a signing of her memoir, *Life in Motion: An Unlikely Ballerina.* The book is a "Cinderella story," sharing the challenges and successes that have brought her to ABT's stage.

• • • • • • • • • • • • • • • • • • • •

The book was honored with the 2015 Coretta Scott King Illustrator Award, the 2015 Ezra Jack Keats Book Award New Writer Honor, and the Essence Magazine Best Children's Book of 2014. Among the many rave reviews, NPR Staff Picks, For Art Lovers, Kids' Books, calls *Firebird*

Vivid and emotional. Copeland's writing and Myers' art draw you into a beautiful world, rich with color, texture and drama. For all budding young artists who maybe don't have role models they can relate to, this little book provides some inspiration.[11]

Meeting Doug Copeland Sr.

In 2002, Misty Copeland represented ABT at the Princess Grace Foundation dance competition. She performed a pas de deux with dance partner Craig Salstein and a flower girl variation from *Don Quixote*. She didn't win, but it was a great opportunity for her to show ABT what she could do. Copeland was maturing as a dancer with the corps. As she developed, her confidence grew. And it was at this time that she made the decision that she was ready to meet her father, Doug Copeland Sr.

Her brother, Doug Jr., had already been in contact with their father for some time. Copeland and her brother came up with a plan. In August 2004, during a break from ABT, both flew to Wisconsin. It was a warm reunion between father and daughter. They shared stories, and she met a few other family members. She also learned about the difficulties her father experienced after Misty's mother left with the children so many years ago. Doug Sr. watches his daughter perform whenever ABT is in Chicago, Illinois.[12]

Endorsements

Copeland has not only mastered ballet but has used what she's learned from dance to become a savvy businessperson. People are inspired by her story of humble beginnings, hard work, and success. In fact, this has become her brand. A brand is the identifying "personality" of a person, organization, product, or service. Copeland's brand is seen in endorsements on television, in print publications, and online. She has represented companies such as American Express, Coach, and Diet Dr. Pepper. Seiko, the watch company, hired Copeland to promote its Progress to Seiko

Copeland celebrated the beauty, strength, and athleticism of ballet in Under Armour's 2014 "I Will What I Want" campaign. Viewers were encouraged to overcome challenges and rejections in order to achieve their dreams.

Campaign.[13] Commercials and print pieces featured the tagline: "Progress: Inspired by beauty, with the strength to shine." The ABT principal dancer was an inspiration for the Seiko Tressia Misty Copeland limited-edition watch. Its elegant design features a diamond-studded bezel and a face made from mother-of-pearl. The watchband is made from rose-gold and silver colored metals. It is solar-powered and comes in pink packaging.[14]

One of Copeland's most notable endorsements was Under Armour's "I Will What I Want" campaign in 2014. At the time, Copeland was a soloist. As Copeland

performs powerful chaines (a series of turns), battements (big kicks), and grand jetes (leaps), a rejection letter is read. It thanked the then thirteen-year-old Misty for applying to its ballet academy but indicates that she wouldn't be accepted. The letter reads that she "lacked the right feet, Achilles tendons, turnout, torso length, and bust." She was told that her body was wrong for ballet, and that at her age, she was too old to be considered. "I Will What I Want" was the tagline.

Signage was also a part of the Under Armour campaign. Copeland is seen with professional athletes. Valerie Block of CNBC .com quotes Copeland as saying, "Dancers are athletes, and it's even harder because we have to add an artistic level and make it look effortless." The

> "Copeland's Under Armour video went viral and has more than eleven million views to date."

principal continues by noting that dancers and athletes are not considered the same. But Under Armor is changing that. Copeland continues, "Putting me up there next to Cam Newton and Stephen Curry was a beautiful thing, showing a woman could be seen equally as strong and powerful as a guy."[15]

MindLeaps

Having experienced poverty as a child, Copeland was particularly honored to team up with MindLeaps in 2015. MindLeaps is a nonprofit humanitarian organization that uses dance and academics to help children. They travelled to Kigali, the capital city of

Rwanda. This African nation was still recovering from a 1994 genocide. Its communities are still rebuilding, trying to establish employment. Education has become less important as families focus on survival. Many children are homeless, do not have access to school, and lack communication skills. The people at MindLeaps knew that they could reach the children through dance.

Children ages nine through eighteen learned technique, as well as traditional academics. As they moved to the music, their cognitive skills began to develop. They also gained the experience to enter into more structured learning environments. English and IT classes were also added, giving the students skills that would prepare them for school or a work environment.

In the past, MindLeaps worked only with male students. But with Copeland's involvement, females were added. She helped to launch the MindLeaps Girls Program. She taught them a basic ballet class. "Dance is giving them hope, a goal, a real escape," Copeland writes in an email to PointeMagazine.com's Amy Brandt. "They are connecting their memory, using their brain for physical coordination, using their words to describe what they're doing and creating." The ballerina also awarded a top student with the Misty Copeland Scholarship. This scholarship allowed the student to attend boarding school. The winner was a young boy who later showed Copeland where he slept—a concrete tunnel under the street. "Dance sets you up for life in the most beautiful way," Copeland says in Brandt's article, "and my time at MindLeaps was the most extreme truth of that."

A Triumphant Return in *A Ballerina's Tale*

A Ballerina's Tale (2015), a documentary directed by Nelson George, portrays Copeland's journey from the *Firebird* success, through her injury, and to her triumphant return. The film turns the spotlight on three important issues in ballet, according to ABallerinasTale.com:

> [T]he absence of women of color at major companies despite so many gifted black women ready to make the leap; the emphasis on skinny bodies for ballerinas impacts the health of professional dancers and sends a negative message to young fans around the world. Misty, because of her race and her curves, is central to both issues in the classical dance world.

ABallerinasTale.com notes that the documentary depicts "how a great talent and a powerful will combined can open doors within a very cloistered world." The film premiered in April at the 2015 Tribeca Film Festival and then opened in October 2015 in New York City.

CHAPTER SEVEN

She Did It!

· · · · · · · · · · · · · · · ·

Although there had been a few African American principal ballerinas in major American ballet companies (Debra Austin for Pennsylvania Ballet in 1982, and Lauren Anderson for Houston Ballet in 1990), Misty Copeland had her eyes set on being the first African American female principal at a major international company.[1] And on June 30, 2015, she realized her dream. She had attended her regular Tuesday company class. Afterward, McKenzie turned to Copeland and asked her to "take a bow." That's it. Simple, but meaningful. Misty Copeland was the first African American woman to be promoted to principal ballerina in the company's seventy-five-year history.[2]

The promotion signified Copeland's mastery of the art form, and it afforded her the chance to take her place in ballet history.[3] As she wrote on Today. com, "The patience that I've had to wait sixteen years before I rose to principal dancer—it's very rare to wait that long—and the hard work I've put in is so beautiful. More so than just something that comes naturally to you or something that's given to you."[4] And yet, Copeland is quick to credit those who came before her and credit those who helped her get to where she is today.

It's About *Time*

In April 2015, Misty Copeland was named one of *Time* magazine's 100 Most Influential People. In a simple unitard, she graced the issue's cover. Copeland's childhood hero, Nadia Comaneci, wrote the feature article, calling Copeland a pioneer. Comaneci also penned an April 16, 2015, article for TimeMagazine .com, writing of Copeland:

> Misty proves that success is not about how you grow up or the color of your skin. Her story—of overcoming personal and physical challenges to become a soloist at the American Ballet Theatre— is the story of someone who followed her dreams and refused to give up. In that way, she is a model for all young girls.[5]

Copeland appeared at the *Time* 100 gala and was quoted by Time.com's Charlotte Alter as saying, "Something that my mother instilled in me, as a biracial woman herself, and me being biracial, was that the world was going to view me as a black woman, no matter what I decided to do." Copeland notes that she is "here to be a vessel for all these brown ballerinas who have come before me."

She strives to set an example of what a ballerina can be and to represent the diversity in the world. She recognized that ABT helps with that, as it works to represents the diversity of a nation, and proves that people can reach their goals if they work hard and have support. Copeland expresses her hope to see more diversity on stage as well as in the audience. Because after all, it is at the ballet that one can dream. In the *Time* video, "Misty Copeland on Changing the Face of Ballet," she says, "I would want a younger child, looking at me on the cover, to see themselves; to see endless opportunities; to see possibilities that maybe they never even thought were something that they could attain. I want them to be able to see dreams through me."[6]

> "Television loves Copeland. She has appeared on *60 Minutes, CBS Sunday Morning,* and *The Today Show.*"

A Broadway Baby

Sometimes ballerinas venture out into other types of dance. In August 2015, Copeland debuted as subway poster girl Miss Turnstiles/Ivy Smith in the Broadway revival of *On the Town*. This musical, by Leonard Bernstein, Adolph Green, and Betty Comden, thrills audiences with the story of three sailors on leave in New York City. Copeland's numbers were based on original choreography by renowned choreographer Jerome Robbins. Copeland played the role from August 25 to September 6, 2015. Her debut received

favorable reviews, including the following from NYTimes.com's Gia Kourlas:

Ms. Copeland, perhaps because she holds her body more rigidly, triumphed in that opening Miss Turnstiles number, in which football players toss Ivy overhead as her legs open in a straddle. (If only it had been danced on point instead of in soft slippers!) Drawing on her own formidable power as the male ensemble manipulated her through a tangle of overhead flips and hand-to-hand walks, Ms. Copeland, with sweet humor, sailed through them and landed on their shoulders with her arms raised in victory. This was her number; she owned it.[7]

Copeland expands her learning and experiences by performing other styles of dance. In 2015, she took up musical theater. Copeland's debut performance of Broadway's *On The Town* took place in New York City's Lyric Theatre on August 25, 2015.

Glamour magazine's twenty-fifth Anniversary Women of the Year Awards highlighted achievements of female trailblazers from a wide variety of industries, such as business, politics, entertainment, and more.

Copeland spoke at the 2015 Glamour Women of the Year Awards in New York City. In her speech, Copeland shared that women are essential to ballet. She also noted that mentors were essential to her being Misty Copeland.

It was held on November 9, 2015, at Carnegie Hall in New York City. Copeland was among the women who blazed their own paths. She shared the stage with other honorees, including Caitlyn Jenner, Victoria Beckham, Cecile Richards, Elizabeth Holmes, Reese Witherspoon, the Women of Charleston, and the US Women's National Soccer Team.[8]

Coming Home Again

Copeland returned to San Pedro, California, in December 2015 for the dedication of the Misty Copeland Square. This area is at the intersection near the San Pedro Dance Center, the school in which Copeland got her training from Cindy and Patrick Bradley. They were in attendance, along with their son Wolf, Misty's former roommate. The program consisted of speeches and the unveiling of a mural by artist Kelcey Fisher. The four paintings were of Copeland and over eighty dancers from San Pedro Dance Center. After a warm embrace with Copeland, Wolf performed a song that he composed specifically for this event, "Wait for Me." Dancers from the San Pedro Dance Center performed while he played and sang.

Copeland then taught a master ballet class at the Warner Grand Theatre in downtown San Pedro. Fifty dancers between the ages of eight and seventeen took part. Greg Autry of LASplash.com details Copeland's patient approach, saying, "She walked through the class stopping to work with individuals, pointing out that the difference between average and professional was in the very basics of dance, and in the little things." Autry continues: "Misty emphasized basics and precision, and teaching the muscles to move reflexively as opposed to physically. She implored the dancers to let their bodies 'sing with the music.'" Proceeds were given to the San Pedro

> "My confidence was really born out of a naivete about the predjudices that colored the world of ballet." [10]

City Ballet Outreach Program, which gives homeless and low-income students the opportunity to train, much like Copeland did as a young teenager. [9]

A Presidential Chat

On February 29, 2016, Copeland, US president Barack Obama, and *Time*'s Maya Rhodan teamed up to discuss race, gender, and achievements. Obama explained that as a father, he's always on the lookout for "strong women who are out there who are breaking barriers and doing great stuff." Copeland is an example of one of these women who have "entered a field that's very competitive, where the assumptions are that she may not belong. And through sheer force of will and determination and incredible talent and hard work she was able to arrive at the pinnacle of her field. And that's exciting."

Rhodan expressed that both Obama and Copeland represented the African American community in their own special way. She asked, "Do you ever think that— how does race come to play? Do you think that people

Barbie Honors Female Role Models

Recognized for the inspiration she offered to children everywhere, Copeland's likeness was created into a Barbie doll![11] The doll was a part of Barbie's "Sheroes" program honoring female role models who have broken through boundaries to pursue their dreams. As a thirteen-year-old, Copeland played with Barbie dolls. She was very shy, and she tells Bill Chappell of NPR.org that Barbie dolls gave her "a way to dream." She explains, "Barbie can transform into anything."[12] When given this opportunity, Copeland recognized its importance. She tells Valerie Block of CNBC.com, "I immediately thought: OK, we have to get this right. We have to really show people what a brown Barbie looks like—what a ballerina Barbie looks like. That she has muscles and is true to who I am." Copeland continues, "Especially in the African American community, it's important for girls to see a positive image of a black woman. I'm proud to represent that."[13] The doll's face resembles Copeland's, and its body is lean and muscular. The costume resembles that of the Firebird with a red unitard, tail, and pointe shoes. On the doll's head sits a dramatic tulle headpiece. The Barbie was released for sale in May 2016.

still treat you differently because of race? Because you're African American?" Copeland responded by saying that the treatment hasn't been direct. It's much more subtle than that, but it's there. She can feel it, and she tries not to get weighed down by the superficial. She just works to be the best dancer she can be, using any obstacles or challenges to fuel her drive. And now more than ever she has a platform on which to use her voice to tell others that it's OK for ballerina's to "have any skin complexion, to have a healthy body image." Copeland believes her voice forces "a lot of these top tier companies to address the lack of diversity and diversifying the bodies that we're seeing in classical ballet." When asked what their "single greatest fixable obstacle to the success of young people today?" Copeland said:

> [B]eing able to have an understanding of yourself and how you fit into society and who you are. But to be empathetic to everyone around you I think is such a powerful thing to hold. To be able to forgive. All of those things I think can strengthen this generation of our youth. I think having a strong sense of self and just knowing who they are and being comfortable with that.[14]

The View from the Top

Copeland appeared as a guest editor for the May 2016 issue of *Dance Magazine*. Jennifer Stahl of DanceMagazine.com wrote, "Why Misty? Because she's got a perspective like no one else in the dance world today, and we wanted to get her view from the very top of the field." Copeland offered story ideas that included: "a feature on what to do when your director tells you to lose weight [something Misty has experienced herself], to how dancers can treat their career more like a business, to a Q&A with Mia Michaels about revamping the Rockettes' New York Spectacular." Stahl was impressed with Copeland as they worked together. She writes:

> No wonder this woman is so successful. She is one of the most determined, yet generous dancers I've ever met. She'll work as hard as she can until she gets things right, but she's completely open to trying new ideas. It's clear why everyone from Under Armour to Prince

Copeland unveiled her new Barbie doll in 2016. It was designed to inspire young people to become anything they'd like, especially in classical ballet. Misty hopes that her life story encourages young people to never give up.

hires her—in addition to her exceptional dance talent, she's simply an incredible collaborator.

Jayme Thornton, the photographer on the project, expressed his/her take on the collaboration on Instagram (@jaymethornton). Thornton shared that ideas flowed freely from Copeland, especially when challenges arose. Copeland was completely open to discussing her professional goals and "even indulged in some birthday cake we brought to her cover shoot, which happened to fall on the birthdays of both our photographer Jayme Thornton and makeup artist Angela Huff."[15]

Wedding Bells are Ringing

On July 31, 2016, Misty Copeland and Olu Evans exchanged wedding vows at the Montage Hotel in Laguna Beach, California. The ballerina and corporate attorney had been dating for ten years. When she appeared at the Soledad O'Brien & Brad Raymond Starfish Foundation's PowHERful Summit, Copeland shared the following with summit host Soledad Obrien:

It took me finding a person that respected me, that allowed me to still fulfill what i [sic] wanted in my career. That was most important to me. I always said "no man is coming in and taking me away from ballet." And that was so important to me that the person I ended up with was going to support me in every way, because my career is so important to me. And I knew immediately

Misty Copeland poses with Olu Evans in July 2015. Shortly after this photograph was taken, Evans proposed to Copeland. The couple was married in 2016, after dating for ten years.

when he wasn't afraid of hearing or seeing me so damaged—and that he wanted to help because he cared about me as a person.[16]

Evans had asked Copeland to be his wife in August 2015, shortly after she achieved her long-time goal of becoming an ABT principal dancer. She had a year full of achievements, but getting married was the icing on the cake. One hundred guests were in attendance at their wedding, all watching the elite ballerina wear a dress designed by Inbal Dror and shoes by Christian Louboutin.

CHAPTER EIGHT

Misty Copeland Out Loud

· · · · · · · · · · · · · ·

Copeland's next act was creating her own dancewear line, Égal. Designed for all bodies, it debuted in August 2016. The inspiration for the line stemmed from her own struggle to find supportive leotards when she was an awkward teen. And the continuation of this business is in great part a tribute to her own hard work. Like dancers everywhere, Copeland worked hard, made sacrifices, and practiced discipline to achieve her dreams. And these were tools she used in working her business. Valerie Block of CNBC.com, notes Copeland's thoughts on the matter:

> Celebrities today make all this money and have all this time to travel and play, go to clubs and get in trouble. But there's never a moment that a dancer can take off and just be like, woo hoo, I'm enjoying all of the applause that I got in my last show! The work never ends until you retire,

In November 2016, Copeland traveled to Havana, Cuba, as part of the US Department of State Sports and Cultural Envoy program. She shared her story, promoted cultural dialogue, and connected with teachers and students training in Cuba.

• •

and I think that having that structure in place as a classical dancer has really benefited me as a businesswoman.[1]

Copeland advises those with aspirations to succeed in any facet of life with the following: "You can't make a wrong decision. Every obstacle and every hardship and every injury has made me into the dancer and the artist that I am today."[2]

Peg + Cat

On October 19, 2016, Misty Copeland guest starred in PBS's animated preschool series *Peg + Cat*. In "The Dance Problem" episode, Copeland helps to tell the story of an aspiring dancer who has overcome various challenges.[3] That same day she appeared on the television show *Good Morning America* to share a bit about her role on the episode. One of Copeland's lines that resonated with her is, "Dancing isn't about how you look, Cat. It's about how you make people feel, and your dancing makes me feel totally awesome."[4]

Peg + Cat was a good challenge for Copeland. She couldn't use dance to tell the story, but rather voiceover and song. She tells Michael Logan of TVInsider.com that she would have watched the episode as a youth and continues by saying:

> No dancers looked like me when I was growing up, so I connected with female singers. Music was a big thing in our household—soul, pop, R&B. Mariah Carey, a biracial woman, was a huge influence on seven-year-old me, and the only public figure I felt I really connected with. She kind of looked like me. When I watched Mariah, I could see there was a place for me in the world. All children need that. They need to see themselves in others. To have a brown ballerina representing the dance world in a cartoon series kids love is an incredibly cool thing.[5]

Worth a Thousand Words

They say a "picture is worth a thousand words," and Copeland is no exception. She has appeared in countless photos, several books, and a calendar.

Captured in Four Years

The first was *Misty Copeland,* a coffee table book by award-winning photographer Gregg Delman. After seeing Copeland in a magazine, Delman reached out to her manager, asking if the dancer would be interested in being photographed.[6] Copeland agreed, and they worked together on a series of images from 2011 through 2014. Copeland wrote the following in the foreword of the book: "Because of the unassuming simplicity in our preparation, I didn't expect to see the exceptional classic beauty that was consistently created in our photographs, and I was blown away by how full and finessed the end product always was." She continues: "For the majority of our shoots there was no glam squad or walls of wardrobe—I did my own hair and makeup, wore my own clothes, and just like that, we'd get to work."[7] *Misty Copeland* was released for sale on September 27, 2016.

Getting the Wrinkles Out

When Copeland appeared in Delman's book, she received flack for some of the images. Rumors flew that her body had been photoshopped in a photo in which she was sitting on her feet wearing a white leotard. She set the record straight by publicizing two versions of the same photo. ABCNews.go.com quotes the ballerina as saying:

The positive body image that is shown throughout is a healthy one and what I stand for. The image on the left was photoshopped to smooth out my leotard. No altering was done to my body. I'm happy and proud of my body and would never participate in changing it.

> "Finding your power doesn't have to be scary. Instead, it makes you feel in control, strong, and proud." [8]

Copeland adds:

[W]hen you're on social media the youth are seeing such horrible imagery of what they think they should have to look like and so, it was really important for me, with this book ... [has] photographs of my body and all that it takes to become a ballerina and the art in what goes into making this body.[9]

Power and Grace in Pictures

Copeland also appeared in Richard Corman's book *Misty Copeland: Power and Grace.* Corman is a well-known portrait photographer and has worked with influential subjects such as Madonna, Muhammad Ali, Michael Jordan, Nelson Mandela, Isamu Noguchi, Meryl Streep, and Kurt Vonnegut. Corman had been told about a piano that had washed ashore just under the enormous Brooklyn Bridge. With camera in hand—as was always the case—he went out to see for himself.

Sure enough, a Mason & Hamlin grand piano was sitting on some sand. He knew the setting was stunning and reached out to Copeland. She enthusiastically agreed to meet the photographer at the site the following day at 5:30 in the morning, despite her packed rehearsal and performance ABT schedule. The photography experience was organic. Copeland showed up with her enthusiasm, hair and make up done, and a simple outfit made up of a black leotard and pointe shoes. They worked in silence. Copeland seemed to "sense" the energy and sound of the piano. Basking in the sunlight, she sat, leaned, and stood en pointe. Corman posted the images on his website and decided to publish *Misty Copeland: Power and Grace* a month later. It was released on July 31, 2015. Corman wrote the following for the Huffington Post:

> I am moved how humility, decency, grace, beauty, brilliance, imagination, discipline and foresight have given Misty a voice that is resounding and speaks volumes about her drive to make a difference in the world today. Her talent is genius and her generous soul is equal to that ability. As her fame skyrockets, it seems her benevolence and accessibility also expands . . . so rare in our world of celebrity.
>
> Young girls of all colors aspire to her voice and talent, as Misty is transforming the hue of classical

ballet by her own example. In being named the first African-American female promoted to principal dancer at the American Ballet Theatre, she has bypassed all the stereotypes of classical ballet and in doing so, has inspired so many. Her growing fame as a dancer clearly gives her this platform, but like visionaries past, she has accepted this role and demanded that others listen.[10]

The rest of the book portrays Copeland in black-and-white in different settings and outfits. Also included were inspiring messages from Copeland, as well as an introduction by Cynthia Bradley. Some of the Copeland photos were compiled in Corman's 2017 wall calendar of the same title.

Barrier Breakers

Annie Leibovitz is a portrait photographer, and in 1999, she was in search of female leaders who span a wide range of industries: CEOs, leaders of companies, artists, politicians, and athletes. She wanted to spotlight these leaders in her "Women" series, noting that they broke barriers in their prospective areas of interest. It was a project she and partner Susan Sontag began in the late 1990s. She then added new subjects, which represented today's growing number of influential women in high positions.

Today "Women: New Portraits" features photos from 1999 and 2016, as well as few in between. Subjects included Misty Copeland, Jane Goodall, Hillary Clinton, Caitlyn Jenner, Adele, Sheryl Sandberg, and

Disney's *The Nutcracker*

In 2016, Disney announced that it was going to make a live-action version of the classical ballet *The Nutcracker*. Lasse Hallström, of *The Hundred-Foot Journey* (2014), *Hachi: A Dog's Tale* (2009), *Chocolat* (2000), and *What's Eating Gilbert Grape* (1993), was hired to be the director. Ashleigh Powell wrote the screenplay, which was based on E.T.A. Hoffmann's short story "The Nutcracker and the Mouse King." Disney's version will be titled *The Nutcracker and The Four Realms*.[12]

Misty Copeland will be the lead ballerina, not being a stranger to the role of Clara. She joins actors Keira Knightley, Morgan Freeman, Helen Mirren, and Mackenzie Foy. Copeland shared the news on her Instagram account. The film is slotted for a 2018 release.

the Williams sisters. Each photo exposes true diversity not limited by role or preconceived ideas. Leibovitz's series made its way around the world, stopping in Frankfurt, Hong Kong, London, Mexico City, Milan, New York, San Francisco, Singapore, Tokyo, and Zurich. A public talks series, called "Women for Women," went along with the tour, discussing topics such as women's rights. Social media users were also invited to share images of inspirational women using the hashtag #ShareYourHero.[11]

A Ballerina Body

Copeland recognized that a shift has occurred in what women consider desirable in their figures. No longer are super thin physiques preferred. Instead, they want a elongated, well-toned physique that is strong and powerful, in essence a ballerina's body. In her book *Ballerina Body: Dancing and Eating Your Way to a Leaner, Stronger, and More Graceful You,* Copeland tells readers how to transform their bodies into a work of art that is lean, strong, and flexible. She includes a fitness regimen based on long-standing ballet exercises. An eating plan details the importance of making good food choices. Copeland also adds in meal plans, a peek into her personal journal, inspiration, and advice on how to find and become a mentor. *Ballerina Body* hit shelves in March 2017.[13]

To Follow in Her Pointe Shoes

These days, Misty Copeland is approached by so many young ballet dancers of all shapes, sizes, and shades. They want to follow in her "pointe shoes," to pursue a career in the art form. Copeland cheers them on and encourages them to jump in and make their way in the ballet world. There is room for each of them. In fact, she remembers what her first ballet teacher, Cynthia Bradley, taught her, that "ballet was richer when it embraced diverse shapes and cultures." Throughout her career, Copeland sometimes struggled to remember this piece of wisdom. But she always came back to it, to this bit of knowledge: "The stage on which I performed was brighter for having me, even

Misty Copeland's dedication, countless rehearsal hours, and inner strength helped her to find her place in ballet. Today, she dances the role of a lifetime as the first African American woman to be promoted to principal ballerina in the ABT's seventy-five-year history.

if some in the audience or dancing beside didn't always agree."[14]

Copeland's dedication in the face of adversity sends a powerful message of not giving up on one's dreams. It also sets the stage for the next generation to further develop the art form she has given her life to share. This is what makes her one of the most influential public figures in the world.

Chronology

1982 Misty Danielle Copeland is born in Kansas City, Missouri.

1997 Misty wins first place at the Music Center Spotlight Awards.

1998 Misty studies at the San Francisco Ballet School.

1999 Misty attends ABT's Summer Intensive.

2000 Misty is named ABT's National Coca-Cola Scholar and is guaranteed a spot with the Studio Company after her high school graduation. She joins ABT's Studio Company.

2001 Copeland joins ABT as a member of the corps de ballet.

2002 Copeland represents ABT at the Princess Grace Foundation dance competition.

2007 Copeland is promoted to soloist for ABT.

2011 *Essence* names Copeland as one of its 37 Boundary-Breaking Black Women in Entertainment.

2012 Copeland is inducted into the Boys & Girls Club National Hall of Fame in San Diego. She is honored with the Breakthrough Leadership Award by the Council of Urban Professionals.

2013 Copeland is named National Youth of the Year Ambassador for the Boys & Girls Clubs of

America. She receives the Young, Gifted & Black honor at the 2013 Black Girls Rock! Awards.

2014 Copeland's *New York Times* best-selling memoir, *Life in Motion: An Unlikely Ballerina*, is released. She is appointed to the President's Council on Fitness, Sports, and Nutrition. She helps with the launch of ABT's Project Plié. She dances the lead role of Odette/Odile in *Swan Lake*. She is featured in Under Armour's "I Will What I Want" campaign. She receives an honorary doctor of fine arts degree from the University of Hartford.

2015 Misty Copeland is named one of *Time* Magazine's 100 Most Influential People, and appears on the magazine cover. She teams up with MindLeaps, a nonprofit humanitarian organization. She is featured in the documentary *A Ballerina's Tale*. She debuts in the Broadway revival of *On the Town*. She is recognized at *Glamour* magazine's 25th Anniversary Women of the Year Awards. She becomes the first African American woman to be promoted to ballerina in ABT's seventy-five-year history.

2016 Copeland becomes a guest editor for the May 2016 issue of *Dance Magazine*. Her likeness is created into a Barbie doll for Barbie's Sheroes program. Misty Copeland and Olu Evans get married. She releases her dancewear line, Égal.

2017 Copeland's *Ballerina Body: Dancing and Eating Your Way to a Leaner, Stronger, and More Graceful You* is released.

Chapter Notes

Chapter 1: A Ballerina is Born

1. Greg Autry, "Misty Copeland Comes Home—Love and Magic Flow in a Master Ballet Class," LASplash .com, http://www.lasplash.com/publish/Los_Angeles_ Charities_188/misty-copeland-comes-home_printer. php.

2. Misty Copeland, *Life In Motion: An Unlikely Ballerina*, New York, NY: Touchstone, 2014.

3. Ibid.

4. Ibid.

5. Ibid.

6. Ibid.

7. "Nadia Comaneci," BartandNadia.com, http://www. bartandnadia.com/index.php?nadia-comaneci.

8. Misty Copeland, *Life In Motion: An Unlikely Ballerina*, New York, NY: Touchstone, 2014.

9. Erin Staley, *Defeating Stress and Anxiety*, New York, NY: The Rosen Publishing Group, Inc., 2016.

10. Copeland, *Life In Motion*.

11. Ibid.

12. Ibid.

Chapter 2: Becoming a "Bun Head"

1. Misty Copeland, *Life In Motion: An Unlikely Ballerina,* New York, NY: Touchstone, 2014.

2. Ibid.

3. Ibid.

4. Ibid.

5. Ibid.

6. Ibid.

7. Bill Chappell, "Misty Copeland Inspires A Barbie 'Sheroes' Doll," NPR.org, May 2, 2016, http://www.npr.org/sections/thetwo-way/2016/05/02/476486268/misty-copeland-inspires-a-barbie-sheroes-doll.

8. Copeland, *Life In Motion.*

9. "Misty Copeland Breaks Ballet's Glass Ceiling," Glamour Magazine, published on Nov 9, 2015, https://www.youtube.com/watch?v=J9BIBGD0XoA.

10. "George Balanchine," The George Balanchine Trust, http://balanchine.com/george-balanchine/.

11. "George Balanchine," NYCBallet.com, https://www.nycballet.com/Explore/Our-History/George-Balanchine.aspx.

12. Ibid.

13. "Mikhail Baryshnikov Biography," Biography.com, http://www.biography.com/people/mikhail-baryshnikov-9201142#synopsis.

14. "Baryshnikov Arts Center Artistic Director Mikhail Baryshnikov," Baryshnikov Arts Center, http://bacnyc. org/about/mikhail-baryshnikov.

15. "Misty Copeland Biography," Bio, August 1, 2016, http://www.biography.com/people/misty-copeland.

Chapter 3: A Dream in the Making

1. Misty Copeland, *Life In Motion: An Unlikely Ballerina*, New York, NY: Touchstone, 2014.

2. "Company History," ABT.org, http://www.abt.org/ insideabt/history.asp.

3. Ibid.

4. Copeland, *Life In Motion*.

5. "Gelsey Kirkland," ABT.org, http://www.abt.org/ education/archive/choreographers/kirkland_g.html.

6. Copeland, *Life In Motion*.

7. "Paloma Herrera: Principal Dancer," ABT.org, http:// www.abt.org/dancers/detail.asp?Dancer_ID=28.

8. Copeland, *Life In Motion*.

9. Copeland.

10. Ibid.

11. Ibid.

12. Ibid.

13. Ibid.

14. Ibid.

15. "Battle Over Misty Copeland Draws Media," TheFreeLibrary.com, December 1, 1998, https://www.

thefreelibrary.com/BATTLE+OVER+MISTY+COPEL
AND+DRAWS+MEDIA.
-a053280622.

Chapter 4: Taking Her Place On Stage

1. Misty Copeland, *Life In Motion: An Unlikely Ballerina,* New York, NY: Touchstone, 2014.

2. Ibid.

3. Ibid.

4. Ibid.

5. Alex Morris, "Ballerina Misty Copeland On Breaking Barriers and Loving Her Strong Body," Glamour.com, October 15, 2015, http://www.glamour.com/story/misty-copeland.

6. Copeland, *Life In Motion.*

7. Ibid.

8. Morris.

9. Copeland, *Life In Motion.*

10. Morris.

11. Copeland, *Life In Motion.*

12. Morris.

13. Gia Kourlas, "Where Are All the Black Swans?," NYTimes.com, May 6, 2007, http://www.nytimes.com/2007/05/06/arts/dance/06kour.html.

14. Scott Brian, "60 Minutes(subtitles caption)- Misty Copeland," YouTube.com, published August 25, 2015, https://www.youtube.com/watch?v=jHJoQw9xuU8.

15. Margaret Fuhrer, "Web Exclusive—An Interview with Raven Wilkinson," PointeMagazine.com, June 2, 2014, http://pointemagazine.com/inside-pt/issuesjunejuly-2014web-exclusive-interview-raven-wilkinson/.

Chapter 5: Representing the American Dancer

1. "About the Competition," The National Ballet of Canada, https://national.ballet.ca/Productions/2016-17-Season/The-Erik-Bruhn-Prize.

2. Misty Copeland, *Life In Motion: An Unlikely Ballerina,* New York, NY: Touchstone, 2014.

3. "A Brief History of Ballet," PBT.org, http://www.pbt.org/community-engagement/brief-history-ballet.

4. Copeland, *Life In Motion.*

5. Astrida Woods, "Misty's Magic," DanceMagazine.com, September 10, 2012, http://dancemagazine.com/news/Mistys_Magic/.

6. "Nine Artists, 10 Schools Honored with Leonore Annenberg Awards," LeonoreAnnenbergScholarships.org, http://www.leonoreannenbergscholarships.org/.

7. Woods.

8. "Merrill Ashley," ABT.org, http://www.abt.org/education/archive/choreographers/ashley_m.html.

9. Copeland, *Life In Motion.*

10. Woods.

11. Margaret Fuhrer, "Web Exclusive—An Interview with Raven Wilkinson," PointeMagazine.com, June 2, 2014, http://pointemagazine.com/inside-pt/issuesjunejuly-2014web-exclusive-interview-raven-wilkinson/.

12. "Firebird," ABT.org, http://www.abt.org/education/archive/ballets/firebird_ratmansky.html.

13. Woods.

14. "Great Futures Start Here - Boys & Girls Clubs of America PSA," Boys & Girls Clubs of America, YouTube.com, published September 20, 2011, https://www.youtube.com/watch?v=YXVKy2vO9Xg.

15. "Misty Copeland Biography," MistyCopeland.com, http://mistycopeland.com/about/.

Chapter 6: The Talent and Will to Open Doors

1. David Isgur, "Ballet Star Misty Copeland to Teach Master Class and Receive Honorary Degree Today," Unotes.Hartford.edu, November 3, 2014, http://unotes.hartford.edu/announcements/2014/11/2014-11-03-ballet-star-misty-copeland-to-teach-master-class-and-receive-honorary-degree-today.aspx.

2. "President's Council on Fitness, Sports & Nutrition," Fitness.gov, http://www.fitness.gov/.

3. "Read the Full Transcript of TIME's Conversation With President Obama and Misty Copeland," Time.com, March 14, 2016, http://time.com/4254551/president-obama-misty-copeland-transcript/.

4. President's Council on Fitness, Sports & Nutrition," Fitness.gov, http://www.fitness.gov/.

5. "Project Plié," ABT.org, http://www.abt.org/education/projectplie/.

6. "Boys & Girls Clubs of America," ABT.org, http://www.abt.org/education/projectplie/bgca/.

7. "Project Plié," ABT.org, http://www.abt.org/education/projectplie/.

8. Misty Copeland, *Life In Motion: An Unlikely Ballerina,* New York, NY: Touchstone, 2014.

9. Alastair Macaulay, "Review: Misty Copeland Debuts as Odette/Odile in 'Swan Lake,'" NYTimes.com, June 26, 2015, http://www.nytimes.com/2015/06/26/arts/misty-copeland-debuts-as-odette-odile-in-swan-lake.html.

10. Copeland, *Life In Motion.*

11. Misty Copeland, Firebird, Amazon.com, https://www.amazon.com/Firebird-Misty-Copeland/dp/0399166157.

12. Copeland, *Life In Motion.*

13. "Misty Copeland Biography," MistyCopeland.com, http://mistycopeland.com/about/.

14. Misty White Sidell, "Seiko Unveils Misty Copeland Watch Design," WWD.com, July 26, 2106, http://wwd.com/fashion-news/fashion-scoops/seiko-misty-copeland-watch-design-10496553/.

15. Valerie Block, "Misty Copeland's grand leap to ballet megabrand," CNBC.com, June 29, 2016, http://www.cnbc.com/2016/07/29/misty-copelands-grand-leap-from-homelessness-to-ballet-megabrand.html.

Chapter 7: She Did It!

1. Allison Sadlier, "Misty Copeland joins cast of Disney's Nutcracker," EW.com, June 13, 2016, http://www.ew.com/article/2016/07/13/disney-nutcracker-misty-copeland.

2. Alex Morris, "Ballerina Misty Copeland On Breaking Barriers and Loving Her Strong Body," Glamour.com, October 15, 2015, http://www.glamour.com/story/misty-copeland.

3. Scott Brian, "60 Minutes(subtitles caption)- Misty Copeland," YouTube.com, published August 25, 2015, https://www.youtube.com/watch?v=jHJoQw9xuU8.

4. Misty Copeland, "Misty Copeland on why she loves her 'ripped' back: 'I see my strength as beauty'," Today.com, October 18, 2016,

http://www.today.com/series/love-your-body/misty-copeland-why-she-loves-her-ripped-back-t103309.

5. Nadia Comaneci, "The 100 Most Influential People: Misty Copeland," Time.com, April 16, 2015, http://time.com/3823308/misty-copeland-2015-time-100/.

6. Charlotte Alter, "Misty Copeland Becomes First Black Principal Ballerina at American Ballet Theatre," Time.com, June 30, 2015, http://time.com/3941742/misty-copeland-black-principal-dancer/.

7. Gia Kourlas, "Misty Copeland Makes Her Broadway Debut in 'On the Town'," NYTimes.com, August 27, 2015, http://www.nytimes.com/2015/08/27/arts/dance/misty-copeland-makes-her-broadway-debut-in-on-the-town.html?_r=0.

8. "Glamour's Women of the Year 2015: Reese Witherspoon, Victoria Beckham, Misty Copeland, and More Honorees," Glamour.com, October 29, 2015, http://www.glamour.com/story/woty-2015-winners.

9. Greg Autry, "Misty Copeland Comes Home - Love and Magic Flow in a Master Ballet Class," LASplash.

com, http://www.lasplash.com/publish/Los_Angeles_
Charities_188/misty-copeland-comes-home_printer.php.

10. Misty Copeland, *Life In Motion: An Unlikely Ballerina,*
New York, NY: Touchstone, 2014.

11. "Misty Copeland Barbie® Doll," The Barbie Collection,
May 2, 2016, http://www.thebarbiecollection.com/more-
pop-culture-dolls/misty-copeland-barbie-doll-dgw41.

12. Bill Chappell, "Misty Copeland Inspires A Barbie
'Sheroes' Doll," NPR.org, May 2, 2016, http://www.npr.
org/sections/thetwo-way/2016/05/02/476486268/misty-
copeland-inspires-a-barbie-sheroes-doll

13. Valerie Block, "Misty Copeland's grand leap to ballet
megabrand," CNBC.com, June 29, 2016, http://www.
cnbc.com/2016/07/29/misty-copelands-grand-leap-from-
homelessness-to-ballet-megabrand.html.

14. "Read the Full Transcript of TIME's Conversation With
President Obama and Misty Copeland," Time.com, March
14, 2016, http://time.com/4254551/president-obama-
misty-copeland-transcript/.

15. Jennifer Stahl, "Misty Copeland Guest Edits Our May
Issue," DanceMagazine.com, April 13, 2016, http://
dancemagazine.com/news/misty-copeland-guest-edits-
may-issue/.

16. "Olu Evans, Misty Copeland's Husband: 5 Fast Facts
You Need to Know," Heavy.com, http://heavy.com/
entertainment/2016/08/misty-copeland-husband-olu-
evans-wedding-lawyer-taye-diggs-cousin-facebook-page/.

Chapter 8: Misty Copeland Out Loud

1. Valerie Block, "Misty Copeland's grand leap to ballet megabrand," CNBC.com, June 29, 2016, http://www.cnbc.com/2016/07/29/misty-copelands-grand-leap-from-homelessness-to-ballet-megabrand.html.

2. Ibid.

3. Michael Logan, "Ballet Star Misty Copeland 'Toons Up for PBS Kids' Peg + Cat (VIDEO)," TVInsider.com, http://www.tvinsider.com/article/99622/ballet-star-misty-copeland-peg-and-cat-guest-voice-video/.

4. Nicole Pelletiere, "Misty Copeland on Body Image, Photoshopping Rumors: 'I've Never Hid From What I Look Like'," ABC.go.com, http://abcnews.go.com/Entertainment/misty-copeland-body-image-photoshopping-rumors-ive-hid/story?id=42902665.

5. Michael Logan, "Ballet Star Misty Copeland 'Toons Up for PBS Kids' Peg + Cat (VIDEO)," TVInsider.com, http://www.tvinsider.com/article/99622/ballet-star-misty-copeland-peg-and-cat-guest-voice-video/.

6. Stacy Lambe, "First Look: Ballerina Misty Copeland's Natural Beauty Shines in New Photography Book," ETOnline.com, http://www.etonline.com/fashion/198970_misty_copeland_photographed_by_gregg_delman/.

7. Gregg Delman, *Misty Copeland*, New York, NY: Rizzoli, 2016.

8. Richard Corman, *Misty Copeland: Power and Grace,* New York, NY: Michael Friedman Group, 2015.

9. Nicole Pelletiere, "Misty Copeland on Body Image, Photoshopping Rumors: 'I've Never Hid From

What I Look Like," ABC.go.com, http://abcnews. go.com/Entertainment/misty-copeland-body-image-photoshopping-rumors-ive-hid/story?id=42902665.

10. Richard Corman, "Capturing Misty Copeland's Power and Grace," HuffingtonPost.com. Retrieved November 20, 2016. http://www.huffingtonpost.com/richard-corman/ capturing-misty-copelands-power-and-grace_b_7952096. html.

11. Katherine Brooks, "Historic Woman Photographer Pays Stunning Tribute To Other Historic Women," HuffingtonPost.com, November 23, 2016, http://www. huffingtonpost.com/entry/annie-leibovitz-women-portraits_us_5835a98ce4b09b6055ffb3c7?.

12. Allison Sadlier, "Misty Copeland joins cast of Disney's Nutcracker," EW.com, June 13, 2016, http://www.ew.com/ article/2016/07/13/disney-nutcracker-misty-copeland.

13. Misty Copeland, "Ballerina Body: Dancing and Eating Your Way to a Leaner, Stronger, and More Graceful You," Amazon.com, https://www.amazon.com/Ballerina-Body-Dancing-Stronger-Graceful/dp/1455596302/ref=pd_ sim_14_2?_encoding=UTF8&pd_rd_i=1455596302&pd_ rd_r=QVGM0QYAZJW3TKZPZM9E&pd_rd_ w=NTuzX&pd_rd_wg=hcYkD&psc=1&refRID=QVGM0 QYAZJW3TKZPZM9E).

14. "Misty Copeland Biography," MistyCopeland.com, http:// mistycopeland.com/about/.

Glossary

acupuncturist One who has been trained in the Chinese therapy of inserting needles into specific body points to relieve pain.

barre A handrail, either attached to a studio wall or freestanding, that supports dancers as they perform specific exercises and stretches.

boarding school A school that houses students during the academic year.

cardio classes Short for cardiovascular classes, these classes are designed to burn calories and increase endurance.

food stamps Government-issued vouchers that can be exchanged for food.

freelance The process of working for one's self.

genocide The demise of a particular group, because of its politics, ethnicity, or culture.

Gyrotonics classes A series of classes built on the Gyrotonic method (a unique method that strengthens and lengthens muscles, while improving coordination, circulation, and joint mobility).

leotard A form-fitting garmet, similar to a tank swimsuit, that allows a ballet teacher to observe and correct body placement during class.

masseuse A female therapist who massages clients.

metatarsals The five bones between the five toes and the arch of the foot.

MRI (magnetic resonance imaging) A type of imaging, using a magnetic field and radio waves, to view one's internal body tissues via computerized images.

muse One, typically a female, who inspires an artist.

Pilates A physical fitness system developed by Joseph Pilates that uses specially designed equipment and techniques to boost strength and flexibility.

plot The storyline of a piece of art, such as a movie, play, ballet, or book.

pointe shoes Special dance shoes that are worn to enable dancers to perform on the tips of their toes.

repertoire A collection of artistic works, or in the case of ballet, classical or contemporary pieces.

tibia The large bone between the ankle and the knee.

turnout The outward rotation of the legs from the hip, which is needed for ballet technique and performance.

Further Reading

Books

Copeland, Misty. *Ballerina Body: Dancing and Eating Your Way to a Leaner, Stronger, and More Graceful You*. New York, NY: Grand Central Life & Style, 2017.

Copeland, Misty. *Life in Motion: An Unlikely Ballerina*. New York, NY: Touchstone, 2014.

Homans, Jennifer. *Apollo's Angels: A History of Ballet*. New York, NY: Random House Trade Paperbacks, 2011.

Ryals, Lexi, and Erwin Madrid. *Misty Copeland*. New York, NY: Scholastic, 2016.

Websites

American Ballet Theatre (ABT)
http://abt.org/default.aspx
Official ABT website featuring dancer profiles, performances, education, and training, as well as how to support the company

Misty Copeland
http://mistycopeland.com
Misty Copeland's official website

Movies/Videos

A Ballerina's Tale
A documentary about Misty Copeland

The Nutcracker and the Four Realms
Disney's movie version of *The Nutcracker*

Index